Landscapes of
TURKEY
(Bodrum and Marmaris)
a countryside guide

Brian and Eileen Anderson

SUNFLOWER
BOOKS

Dedicated to Ian, Neil, Janet, Paul, Lindsey and Tracey

First published 1991 by
Sunflower Books
12 Kendrick Mews
London SW7 3HG, UK

ISBN 0-948513-67-5

Important note to the reader

We have tried to ensure that the descriptions and maps in this book are error-free at press date. The book will be updated, where necessary, whenever future printings permit. It will be very helpful for us to receive your comments (sent in care of the publishers, please) for the updating of future printings. We also rely on those who use this book — especially walkers — to take along a good supply of common sense when they explore. Conditions change fairly rapidly in Turkey, and *storm damage or bulldozing may make a route unsafe at any time.* If the route is not as we outline it here, and your way ahead is not secure, return to the point of departure. *Never attempt to complete a tour or walk under hazardous conditions!* Please read carefully the notes on pages 41 to 48, as well as the introductory comments at the beginning of each tour and walk (regarding road conditions, equipment, grade, distances and time, etc.). Explore *safely*, while at the same time respecting the beauty of the countryside.

Photographs by the authors
Maps by John Theasby and Pat Underwood
Drawings by Frances Winder
Colour separations by Reed Reprographic, Ipswich
Printed and bound in the UK by KPC Group, Ashford, Kent

✼ Contents

Preface   5
  Acknowledgements; Recommended books   6

Getting about   7

Picknicking   9
  Picnic suggestions   10

Touring   13
  THE BODRUM PENINSULA (TOUR 1)   16
    Bodrum • Turgutreis • Gumusluk • Yalikavak •
    • Mumcular • Comlekci • Guvercinlik •
    Bodrum
  ANCIENT KINGDOMS (TOUR 2)   20
    Bodrum • Heraklia • Priene • Miletus • Euromos •
    Bodrum
  CARIAN INTERIOR (TOUR 3)   24
    Bodrum • Temple of Lagina • Cine Cayi Gorge •
    Alabanda • Alinda • Bodrum
  EPHESUS FROM BODRUM (TOUR 4)   27
    Bodrum • Soke • Selcuk • Ephesus • Bodrum
  **PAMUKKALE ('COTTON CASTLE') FROM BODRUM
  (TOUR 5)**   28
    Bodrum • Yatagan • Mugla by-pass • Denizli •
    Pamukkale • Aphrodisias • Nyssa • Aydin • Bodrum
  THE SERPENTINE RUN (TOUR 6)   32
    Marmaris • Datca • Knidos • Marmaris
  KING CAUNOS AND CLEOPATRA (TOUR 7)   34
    Marmaris • Dalyan • Sedir Adasi • Marmaris
  LYCIAN ADVENTURE (TOUR 8)   36
    Marmaris • Fethiye (Telmessus) • Letoon • Kalkan •
    Xanthos • Patara • Marmaris
  EPHESUS FROM MARMARIS (TOUR 9)   38
    Marmaris • Aydin • Selcuk • Ephesus • Priene •
    Miletus • Heraklia • Euromos • Milas • Yatagan •
    Marmaris
  PAMUKKALE FROM MARMARIS (TOUR 10)   39
    Marmaris • Mugla by-pass • Pamukkale • Aphrodisias
    • Nyssa • Aydin • Marmaris
  **BODRUM TO MARMARIS OR MARMARIS TO BODRUM
  (TOUR 11)**   40
    Bodrum • Milas • Yatagan • Marmaris • Yatagan •
    Milas • Bodrum

Walking   41
  Guides, waymarking, maps   42
  What to take   42

Where to stay   43
Weather   44
Things that bite or sting   44
Turkish for walkers   45
Organisation of the walks   47
A country code for walkers and motorists   48

WALKS FROM BODRUM

1 Akcaalan to Akyarlar   49
2 Gumusluk • Karakaya • Gumusluk   53
3 Yalikavak • Sandima • Geris • Yalikavak   57
4 Yalikavak • Sandima • Yaka • Ortakent   62
5 *Yel degirmenleri* • Sandima • (Geris) • Yaka • Ortakent   66
6 Dagbelen to the Bitez *yolu*   69
7 Gundogan to Dagbelen   73
8 Ortakent • Yaka • Derekoy   76
9 Around and above Konacik   80
10 Konacik • Pedesa • Bodrum   83
11 Kargicak to Labranda and back (the 'Sacred Way')   87

WALKS FROM MARMARIS

12 Beldibi circuit   91
13 Armutalan • Dereozu • *cesme* (Datca *yolu*)   95
14 Armutalan • *orman yolu* • *cesme* (Datca *yolu*)   100
15 Armutalan • Beldebi • Marmaris   102
16 Icmeler to Turunc   105
17 Turunc • Amos • Turunc   109
18 Orhaniye • Castabus • Datca *yolu*   111
19 Datca • Kargi • Armutlu • Datca   115
20 Cetibeli • Camli • Cetibeli   118
21 Cetibeli • *deniz* • Marmaris road   123
22 Akcapinar to Gokce   127
23 Marmaris waterfalls   130

Bus timetables   132

Index   135

Fold-out touring map   between pages 14 and 15
   including plans of Bodrum and Marmaris

Tangerine and bread-sellers, Bodrum

✳ Preface

Tall masts, sun shimmering on sea, boat-filled harbours, castles, minarets, and mosques are inescapable images of Bodrum and Marmaris. But there is more, much more. No part of the world can be more beautiful than the western and southern coasts of Turkey, claims Freya Stark, and this is your opportunity to see if you agree.

Lively and colourful as they are, it is sometimes a pleasure to escape the bustle of these popular resorts, to find solitude in the countryside, and this book shows you just how easy it can be. Although walking is emphasised, the book is not intended solely for walkers. The car tours will get you out and about on voyages of discovery, to visit regions of great natural beauty or historical interest — or maybe for a quiet lunch at some secluded trout farm. If you enjoy the delights of a picnic on holiday, then look at the picnic suggestions, most of which can be reached by public transport and a fairly short walk.

Above all else, Bodrum and Marmaris have one feature in common — they are both gateways to some of the most exciting walking country you can expect to find in the Aegean.

Bodrum offers only a small peninsula to explore, but with the virtue of intimacy. Enjoying shore to shore views, as you wander along some ancient trail across the backbone, it is easy to believe that you are on an island, for there is little to persuade you otherwise. But there is no lack of variety in the landscape. From the rich pastures and pines of the limestone west to the fantastic rugged terrain of the volcanic east, there is scenic interest every step of the way. Nor can you escape the sense of history. The Lelegians occupied the region in early times and left behind eight towns scattered about the peninsula. These unexcavated remains are quietly passing into oblivion. Sometime in the future we would like to return to track them all down but, for the moment, only Pedesa features in our walks. Windmills on the skyline, deserted villages, walled-in footpaths, flowers, and friendly folk may not be your first impressions when you visit Bodrum, but they are likely to be the ones you take home.

The country around Marmaris could hardly be more different. Swathes of green pine cloak the hills, like giant waves frozen in motion, surrounding this one-time fishing village. The Marmaris peninsula has perhaps one of the most convoluted coastlines anywhere in the Aegean, and there is only one way to enjoy it, on foot. Impenetrable the forests may look, but there are footpaths in plenty to set you off in the right direction. Whether you want to find those inviting tiny coves in a wandering coastline, the almost-forgotten ancient theatres, or the fascinating flora of the region, the choice is yours. But if you are set to explore a little further afield, then you'll find Marmaris a good base, and our walks stretch as far as Datca in the west and Akcapinar in the east.

It hardly matters whether you choose Marmaris or Bodrum for your first holiday in Aegean Turkey. The countryside is so beautiful in these parts that it is impossible not to be lured back again and again — with us, we hope, as your constant companions!

Acknowledgements

To the many new friends we made in Turkey, who not only helped us on our way, but often overwhelmed us with hospitality, we say thank you. Our appreciation, too, goes once again to some very good friends: to Enno and Susanne Henke from Frankfurt, for lending support throughout their holidays and lightening the miles with pleasurable companionship and, at home, to Barry and Doreen Boothman for their caring support while we were away and, again, through the less-enviable task of writing.
A special thanks to Gifford Newton & Sons for their Cotswold walking shoes from the High Country range, which served us very comfortably, making the 1600km/1000 miles of walking while researching this book seem almost effortless.

Recommended books

Tom Brosnahan: *Turkey, a travel survival kit* (Lonely Planet)
George E Bean: *Aegean Turkey* (covers the region north of Bodrum, including Ephesus); *Turkey beyond the Maeander* (covers Bodrum and Marmaris) (John Murray)
Freya Stark: *Ionia, a quest* (Century Hutchinson)

☀ Getting about

If you want to see as much as possible of the regions around Bodrum and Marmaris — and there are many ancient sites and much beautiful countryside to savour — then a **hire car** has many advantages. It is convenient and gives you independence and flexibility. But it is expensive. There is often a better deal to be had by booking the hire car before you leave, rather than in Turkey; this can be done through your holiday company or through the major car hire agencies. Sharing the hire car is another way of helping to reduce costs. But you may be on holiday to escape the burden and responsibility of driving, in which case there are plenty of other options to consider.

Taxis are freely available in both Bodrum and Marmaris, but they also tend to be expensive, and they often charge more when the journey takes you over unsurfaced roads (called 'stabilised roads'), which are not uncommon — especially around Marmaris. It pays to establish a price beforehand, if you are contemplating a long journey, and don't hesitate to shop around a little.

Coach and minibus excursions, organised by the bus companies or *dolmus* owners, are plentiful, and these will take you to all the major sites of interest near or far. They represent extremely good value, but take care to choose a coach for a long journey, since these offer a higher standard of comfort. **Boat cruises**, too, are on offer in both Marmaris and Bodrum, but especially so in Marmaris, where small boats (water *dolmus*) ply the harbour area, visiting beaches and islands around the bay. You can use these for specific journeys as well, for instance to get you to and from walks (if they lie on their route), but you will have to negotiate the details yourself. Where water *dolmus* can be conveniently used as transport, this is mentioned in the walk details.

There is no doubt that the most interesting way of getting about is by using the excellent **local transport** (coaches and *dolmus*). This is both efficient and cheap. The operating methods are discussed in some detail in the timetable section, pages 132-134. The town plans on the touring map show you where to find your buses in both Bodrum and Marmaris, but please note that, while there is one station (*otogar*) for both coaches and *dolmus* in

7

Bodrum, Marmaris has only an *otogar* for coaches. The *dolmus* have no proper home in Marmaris, but start from various locations (all of them are shown on the map).

The coaches operate to a regular timetable and serve the long-distance destinations, but they can be used for short hops to get to the start or return you from a walk. Using this reliable and comfortable service, it is easy to plan your own excursion to more distant places of interest — see, for example, the suggestions highlighted (beside a sketch of the two of us) on pages 27 and 39.

The *dolmus* go just about everywhere, and frequently; their destination is displayed in the front window. They do not operate to a strict timetable, but set off when the driver is happy that he has enough people on board. They will stop anywhere on request to pick up and put down, and tickets are not required — just pay the driver as you alight.

There are some rules of politeness to observe if you wish to photograph people in Turkey. To photograph women, you must first seek permission from the men present — simply hold your camera up to indicate your intention. A slight 'tsch' sound, with the head inclined upward and backward, is a refusal. Often, however, the women are keen to have their pictures taken and, if there are no men present, they may even stop you to ask. Somewhere along the way on Walk 5, we chanced upon this old lady on her donkey. She rode upon it in a relaxed manner, bare feet dangling from baggy *shalvar*, head covered with a scarf tied under her chin. Over her shoulder, a string bag dangled before her. We stood aside to give her room to pass, but she stopped and gazed at us. There was no trace of guile, just open child-like curiosity. *'Merhaba'* ('hello'), we greeted her cheerily, and her face changed to warmth and smiles. Questions poured forth. 'Where have you been? Where are you going?' No answers were needed, however; she had spotted our camera and instantly entertained a new idea — a photograph. 'Wait', she asked. The bag was taken off and thrown to the ground, her head scarf was loosened and rearranged. Still sitting astride the donkey, she declared herself ready. She told us her name and address, so that we could send a picture. It was the simplicity of her address, which read 'the meadow, above Geris', which so deeply impressed on us the uncomplicated lifestyle of the people in that part of Turkey.

 Picnicking

There are few official picnic sites offering a full range of facilities in this area of Turkey, but you will find picnic tables situated in beautiful, well-shaded locations along major routes. Some have grills for barbecuing. Picnic tables are more a feature of the wooded Marmaris region, and are rarely seen around Bodrum.

Our picnic suggestions take you to unspoilt, secluded locations along the routes of our walks and some car tours, where you can enjoy the tranquil ambience of the countryside. Most are fairly accessible but, due to their isolation, some require more walking — although getting there is well worth the extra effort involved.

All the information you need to get to these picnic places is given on the following pages, where *picnic numbers correspond to walk numbers*. You can quickly find the general area by looking at the large touring map (where the settings for the walks are outlined in white). We include transport details (🚌 = how to get there by bus; 🚗 = where to leave your private transport), how long a walk you'll have, and views or setting. Beside the picnic title you'll find a map reference; the exact location of the picnic spot, and where to leave your private transport is shown on this large-scale *walking map* by the symbol **P**. Some of the picnic spots are illustrated.

Please remember that if more than a few minutes' walking is required, you will need to wear sensible shoes and to take a sunhat (○ indicates a picnic in full sun). A plastic groundsheet or large plastic bags could be useful, too — especially early in the season, when the ground might still be damp.

If you are travelling to your picnic by bus, refer to the timetables on pages 132-134, but remember that it's always a good idea to get up-to-date timetable information from the bus station or tourist information office. **If you are travelling to your picnic by car**, be extra vigilant off the main roads; children and animals are often in the village streets. Be careful where you park: don't damage the vegetation and flowers, and be sure not to block a road or track.

All picnickers should read the country code on page 48 and go quietly in the countryside.

Picnic food suggestions: It isn't always easy to know what to take on a picnic in a strange country, so here are a few ideas. Buy your *ekmek* (bread) fresh each day from the local bakery, or help yourself from the cabinets outside shops, then pay inside. From the local market and shops buy fresh *salatalık* (cucumber), *domates* (tomatoes), *marul* (lettuce), *zeytin* (olives), *beyaz pınar* (white sheeps' milk cheese), *yoğurt* (yogurt), *bal* (honey) and *lokum* (Turkish delight). There is also a selection of *sosis* (sausage; *sucuk* is Turkish sausage) and cooked meats. *Meyva* (fruit) in season can also be bought. Another possibility is take-away food from cafés and *lokantas*. Choices here are *piliç izgara* (grilled chicken), *şiş kebap* (meat on skewer), *köfte* (meatballs) or even *biber dolması* (stuffed green peppers) from the *meze* counter, where you'll find a wide selection of starters.

If you'd like to have a barbecue (remember, **not** in forested areas, except on official sites), seek out a good butcher's shop where meat is kept on refrigerated display. You won't find familiar cuts of meat, and you'll pay a similar price for best fillet and cheaper cuts. Point and ask for a *yarım* (half) kilo of what will be mainly *kuzu* (lamb) and maybe some *sığır eti* (beef). Say you want *et* (meat *ızgarada* (to grill). Other useful words here are *pirzola* (cutlet), *kıyma* (minced meat), *dilim* (slice), *parça* (piece) — and a very useful word, especially with minced meat, *yağsız* (without fat). The *kasap* (butcher) will bone chickens ready for grilling, if you ask him. Remember, if you feel a little bit uncertain about using the language, just write down your key words and show them to the butcher.

Finally, don't forget something to drink — perhaps *su* (water), *maden suyu* (mineral water), *meşrubat* (soft drinks), or *gazoz* (fizzy drink). Our favourite in this group is *meyva suyu* (fruit juice), which is natural fruit juice and comes in a few varieties; *vişne suyu* (sour cherry) is particularly delicious. Besides being available in bottles, you can buy it in cartons up to a 1-litre size — ideal for picnics. For more heady refreshment, take a bottle of Turkish *şarap* (wine), which is quite palatable, especially if you stick to well-known labels such as Villa Doluca and Kavaklıdere. (We also enjoyed some lesser-known labels.) Choose from *beyaz* (white), *roze* (rose), *kırmızı* (red) or *köpüklü* (sparkling).

Şerefe! (Cheers!)

1 AKYARLAR WINDMILLS (Map page 51) ○

🚗 Park on the approach to Karabağ, where the road is wide. Do not attempt to drive closer as there are no parking opportunities. Follow notes for Walk 1 from the 22min point. **30 minutes on foot**

🚌 *Dolmuş* to Turgutreis; alight at the Akcaalan *yolu* (road), just as Turgutreis comes into sight. Follow Walk 1 as far as the windmills. For a shorter walk, alight at the Karabağ *yolu* (road) nearer Turgutreis. Walk up the road on the left to Karabağ, then pick up the notes for Walk 1 at the 28min-point. **41 or 51 minutes on foot**

A spectacular vantage point with dramatic vistas, but little shade

2a KARAKAYA SADDLE (Map page 54) ○

🚗 Park well into the roadside on the seaward side of Gumusluk inland village, then follow Walk 2. **23 minutes on foot**

🚌 *Dolmuş* to inland Gumusluk, then follow Walk 2 from the starting point. **23 minutes on foot**

The mesmeric effect of Karakaya, clinging to the rocky hillside like some long abandoned film set, will capture your imagination.

2b KARAKAYA WINDMILL (Map page 54; Photograph page 53)

🚗 or 🚌 as Picnic 2a. **26 minutes on foot by car or bus**
*Delightful location, especially when spring flowers adorn the meadow
with a colourful mantle; some shade from the windmill*

3a SARNIC BELOW SANDIMA (Map pages 58-59; Photo page 61)

🚗 Turn left on reaching the square just past the mosque in Yalikavak
and park by the roadside; then follow Walk 3. **20 minutes on foot**
🚌 *Dolmus* to Yalikavak, then follow Walk 3. **20 minutes on foot**
Beautiful views down over Yalikavak and the bay; pastoral setting

3b SANDIMA (Map pages 58-59)

🚗 or 🚌 as Picnic 3a. **30 minutes on foot**
*Large grassy area with some shade on the edge of this absolutely fas-
cinating, almost deserted village (shown in the photograph page 64)*

5 YALIKAVAK SEASCAPE (Map pages 58-59) ○

🚗 From the windmills above Yalikavak, drive to the 9min-point in
Walk 5; then park safely near the corner, off the road if possible. Follow
the notes for Walk 5 from the 9min-point. **20 minutes on foot**
🚌 *Dolmus* to Yalikavak; alight at the windmills, before the descent to
Yalikavak, following instructions for Walk 5. (The *dolmus* does pass the
9min-point recommended for drivers, but it is difficult to ask the driver to
stop, unless you already know the route.) **28 minutes on foot**
Splendid panorama over Yalikavak bay from this secluded location

6 SHADED YAYLA (Map page 74)

🚗 Park by the side of the track at the entrance to Dagbelen and follow
notes for Walk 6 from the 16min-point. **30 minutes on foot**
🚌 *Dolmus* to Yalikavak: alight by the Dagbelen track, just before the
windmills in (5) above; follow notes for Walk 6. **46 minutes on foot**
*Tranquil shaded setting with a timeless quality and views down the
valley to Yukari Golkoy*

7 PINE WOODS (Map page 74)

🚗 Park sensibly off the road near the start of the trail at Gundogan, then
follow notes for Walk 7. **12 minutes on foot**
🚌 *Dolmus* to Gundogan; follow Walk 7. **12 minutes on foot**
*An open grassy area shaded by pine trees with views in the direction of
Gundogan*

9/10 OLD OLIVE GROVE (Map page 85)

🚗 Park by the side of the main road at Konacik, then follow Walk 9.
34 minutes on foot
🚌 *Dolmus* to Konacik (any westbound *dolmus* except Gumbet); then
follow Walk 9. **34 minutes on foot**
*Huge pistachio bushes, unusually formed into neat mounds, dominate
this peaceful oasis cradled in the foothills behind Konacik.*

12a ANCIENT PHYSCUS (Map pages 92-93) ○

🚗 Park where convenient on the Beldibi road, near the 13min-point in
Walk 12, then continue by following those notes. **7 minutes on foot**
🚌 There is no bus connection, but you can walk here from Marmaris
(Walk 12). **20 minutes on foot**
*A place of historical significance in a pastoral setting, affording
unforgettable views over Marmaris*

12b SHADED SADDLE (Map pages 92-93; Photograph page 90)

🚌 Park as for 12a and follow the notes for Walk 12. **17 minutes on foot**
🚍 No bus connection; walk directly from Marmaris. **30min on foot**
Tranquillity and peace make the saddle a place for lingering.

13 RIDGE VIEW (Map pages 92-93) ○

🚌 Park at Armutalan, on the track alongside the electricity substation; then follow notes for walk 13. **22 minutes on foot**
🚍 *Dolmus* to Armutalan; follow Walk 13. **22 minutes on foot**
Elevated, grassy shaded area with panoramic views over Marmaris

14 MARMARIS BAY PANORAMA (Map pages 92-93)

🚌 Park at a convenient point on the main road in Armutalan, near the 5min-point in Walk 14. **25 minutes on foot**
🚍 *Dolmus* to Armutalan mosque, then follow the notes for Walk 14. **30 minutes on foot**
Rocky outcrop overlooking the fjord-like scenery of Marmaris Bay

17 AMOS (Map page 110; Photograph page 108) ○

🚌 Park at Amos, or leave car parked by the mosque in Turunc and follow notes for Walk 17. **No walking — or up to 45 minutes on foot**
🚍 not accessible by bus
Views directly to Marmaris through the entrance to Marmaris Bay

18 CASTABUS (Map page 113)

🚌 Park below Castabus: drive along the track to the 39min-point in Walk 18 or, if you come by jeep, continue up to the site. **27 minutes on foot by car; no walking if you travel by jeep**
🚍 not easily accessible by bus
Superb views over Erine to the Datca peninsula from a ruined temple

19 KARGI BAY (Map page 115) ○

🚌 Park off the track before reaching the beach, unless the track into the parking area by the beach has been improved. **No walking**
🚍 Coach to Datca; follow notes for Walk 19. **40 minutes on foot**
A few unobtrusive buildings scattered along a narrow shingly beach with a crystal-clear sea; small restaurant in summer

20 SECLUDED MEADOW (Map pages 120-121)

🚌 Park by the roadside in Cetibeli. Follow notes for Walk 20 (Short walk 20-1) to the 30min-point. **30 minutes on foot**
🚍 *Dolmus* (Marmaris-Mugla); alight at the trout (*alabalik*) restaurant, as you enter Cetibeli. Follow Walk 20. **30 minutes on foot**
An undisturbed shaded meadow, with views to ruins on a hill

21 HIDDEN YAYLA (Map pages 120-121)

🚌 Park by Cetibeli's new mosque; follow Walk 21. **39min on foot**
🚍 *Dolmus* (Marmaris to Mugla); alight by Cetibeli *yeni* (new) mosque, then follow the notes for Walk 21. **39 minutes on foot**
Lovely enclosed yayla (meadow) in a pine wood

23 OLD MILL (Map pages 92-93; Photograph page 26)

🚌 Park by the roadside, near the junction of Marmaris by-pass and the Mugla road, then follow Walk 23. **14 minutes on foot**
🚍 Not required. Walk from Marmaris. **24 Minutes on foot**
Beautiful shaded glade by ruined mill and pool

❀ Touring

Turkey is a huge country, and distances between the main areas of population are correspondingly great, but an ever-improving road system enables you to cover long distances fairly smoothly and easily. Although the bus service is excellent, hiring a car gives you the freedom to see and savour the varied countryside at your own pace, as well as allowing forays off the beaten track.

Car hire is expensive, and the hire of a jeep even more so, which is a good reason for sharing the cost if possible. Prices tend to double during the main tourist season, but you can still strike a reasonable hire bargain at the beginning and end of the season — if you're prepared to shop around. Sometimes better hire rates can be arranged at home before you travel, especially in high season, and it is worth checking with your holiday company or international car hire agencies.

Take care when renting: before setting out, check the car (have you got a spare tyre, jack, enough petrol; do lights work, etc?), and clarify the **rental conditions** and insurance coverage — take the time, however tedious, to read the terms of the lease. Tyre and windscreen damage are the responsibility of the hirer (including punctures), so check carefully before you drive off, including the spare. If you are unfortunate enough to be involved in an **accident** you must ***not*** move the vehicle, but summon the police, no matter how remote your situation or how seemingly minor the damage. Failure to do this may invalidate your **insurance**. This is normally a condition laid down by the insurance company and a point to check carefully with the hire firm. Don't hesitate to refuse a car if you're not happy with it. Always carry the agency's phone numbers with you, and take some water, food and warm clothing in case of breakdown. The wearing of **seat belts** is compulsory and, even though you may not find many local people complying, they always belt up when they know there's the possibility of a police check.

Petrol stations are frequent along main routes and open seven days a week; these include many of the international companies, some of whom offer a 24-hour service. There are only the occasional petrol stations in more remote areas, and they could have run out of petrol — so

13

don't rely on them for a major fill-up. Some grades of petrol may be unfamiliar: super-normal and regular are self-explanatory; *benzine* = normal; *motorin* = diesel. For **medical** attention, look for the red crescent sign, not the red cross. **Water** sources are very important, in view of the great distances between communities and the very hot summers, and on main roads there are taps by the roadside, their location indicated by a road sign. Off the main road you will also pass water fountains (*çeşme*), but these are not usually indicated. *İçme suyu* = drinking water; *içilir* = drinkable; *içilmez* = not drinkable.

Drive carefully; the road is regarded as a pavement, especially in country areas. Be extra vigilant for animals which are grazed untethered by unfenced main roads, even in the central reservation of dual carriageways! It is not unusual for a herd of goats to flow into the road unexpectedly. Be aware also that roads almost invariably narrow appreciably where they cross bridges, even on wide fast-flowing main roads, and there are usually no warnings. Indeed, a general lack of road signs and road markings can be disconcerting at first, so take extra care. After rain, some stabilised tracks can become slippery and difficult to negotiate, so be extra careful or turn back.

The general standard of driving lacks the discipline to which we are accustomed. For most drivers there is only one lane, and that's the middle of the road. (Lane discipline is, however, better in this region than we've encountered elsewhere in Turkey.) Overtaking on a blind corner or approaching the brow of a hill; driving the wrong way along dual carriageways or one-way streets; ignoring red traffic lights; this is seen all too frequently. In the interests of your own safety, it pays to be aware of this before you start driving in Turkey.

The major towns can be quite congested with traffic, but out on the open road, except for important trunk roads, there is very little traffic. There are frequent **police checks** along main routes outside town, so make sure you have the relevant documents relating to your vehicle, your driving licence, and your passport to hand. Virtually all traffic is stopped, but tourists are mostly waved on. Nevertheless, be prepared!

Remember to take a **pocket phrase book**, if only for the road signs: you won't find any in English. **Ancient sites** are usually indicated by a yellow sign from the main roads. **Telephones** are located in or near post offices; otherwise hotels, *lokantas*, cafés, and shops will let you use their phones at the local rates. **Toilets** are available in most towns, frequently by a mosque; others are found in cafés, *lokantas*, and some petrol stations. Don't rely on toilet paper being supplied; carry your own. Museums and smaller ancient sites are often closed on Mondays, but Ephesus and Pamukkale are open all the time. Enquire at the local tourist office for **opening times** in advance.

The touring notes are brief: they include little history or information about the towns and historical sites. Some literature is available from tourist offices, but it's essential to take a good guide book; see our book list on page 6. We concentrate mainly on the 'logistics' of touring: times and distances, road conditions, viewpoints, and good places to rest. Most of all we emphasise possibilities for **walking** (if you team up with walkers you may lower your car hire costs) and **picnicking** — all the walks and picnics in the book are highlighted, where relevant, in the car tours. If you want to stretch your legs, look at the short walks listed with the main walks, or the picnic suggestions on pages 9 to 12. These short walks will give you a taste of the varied landscapes we explore.

The tours start on the seafront — in Bodrum by the main mosque and in Marmaris by the Ataturk statue. However, you can easily key into them if you are staying at one of the other resorts in the area. **The large touring map is designed to be held out opposite the touring notes** and contains all the information you will need outside Bodrum and Marmaris. (For **town plans**, see the touring map.) **Allow plenty of time for stops**: our times include only short breaks at viewpoints labelled (☎) in the touring notes. Distances quoted are *cumulative km* from Bodrum or Marmaris. A key to the **symbols** in the notes is on the touring map.

It's very difficult to recommend a particular tour **if you only hire a car for one day**. For a long trip from Bodrum, Tour 2 will take you back in time, and you'll certainly enjoy some spectacular scenery around Lake Bafa. If you don't want to drive too far, Tour 1 will surprise you with the varied landscapes to be found on the Bodrum peninsula. A long trip from Marmaris, offering breathtaking, dramatic panoramas, is Tour 6; but for a relatively straightforward run through countryside with a more bucolic appeal, Tour 7 will also entrance you.

All motorists should read the country code on page 48 and go quietly in the countryside.

1 THE BODRUM PENINSULA

Bodrum • Turgutreis • Gumusluk • Yalikavak • Mumcular • Comlekci • Guvercinlik • Bodrum

152km/95mi; about 3 hours 40min driving. Exit Bodrum from main mosque (see town plan on the touring map).

On route: Picnics (see pages 9-12) 1-9; Walks 1-10

On the whole, good surfaced roads are used throughout, but there are a few rough patches, particularly where least expected — on the road from Gundogan to the Milas road junction, so take care. Refer to the enlargement of the Bodrum peninsula beside the large touring map.

This tour is designed to give you an overview, to let you sample some of the delights of the Bodrum peninsula. Visit the timeless fishing village of Gumusluk and enjoy compelling vistas en route. Cruise through pine woods on the old road between Bodrum and Milas. Enjoy typical hospitality in a Turkish village, where the mysteries of carpet-making are divulged over a glass of *cay* (tea).

Leave Bodrum from the square by the main mosque and head up past the bus station to the ring road, where you turn left. Continue on the dual carriageway past the ancient theatre on the right, taking careful note as the dual carriageway ends, and traffic becomes two-way again shortly afterwards. As you drive along you'll probably notice plenty of boat-building activity, before reaching **Konacik**, the starting point for Walks 9 and 10. The road on the left after 6.1km leads to Bitez, from where you can wander through a maze of tangerine groves down to the coast. This junction is also where Walk 6 ends.

After passing the road right to Yalikavak (8.7km), on the approach to **Ortakent** (☀;Walks 4, 5 and 8), you will see a striking line of windmills on a barren hillside and catch glimpses of interesting 17th-century tower houses in the village below (see illustration page 63). Once past Ortakent, the road winds through the villages of **Yahsi** and **Gurece,** with their distinctive minarets, before passing the Gumusluk junction on the right (14.4km). The silver-green olive trees soften an otherwise spartan landscape, and rugged hills close in as you pass through **Islamhanaleri** and soon see Akcaalan ahead. Reach the start of Walk 1 and Picnic 1 on the left (19.6km), just as you crest the hill. As you descend, note the road off left to Karabag, where Short walk 1-1 ends and a shorter version of Picnic 1 begins. On reaching **Turgutreis** (21km ⛵⛵⛟✕⊕⚓M WC), park in the car park on the left — just before the road left to Akyarlar (Walk 1 ends in Akyarlar).

To continue, head back in the direction of Bodrum, but turn left to Gumusluk after 21.9km, just before the petrol station. The narrow surfaced road is quite rough for a couple of minutes, but it improves once you are past **Kadikalesi** (25.4km). This is a pretty run through cultivation which brings a splash of colour, to contrast with the stark hillsides. Reach a T-junction in 28.1km; turn left down to **Gumusluk** ★ (28.7km 🖅🎦🏔🏚✕🚘) by the sea. You must park in the car park on the right; traffic is not allowed along the sea front. This is a gorgeous spot where you're sure to want to linger — and ideal for lunch by the sea (see cover photograph). It is also the site of ancient Myndos and some silver mines (hence the *Gumus*, Turkish for 'silver').

Resume the tour by driving through Gumusluk inland village (30km 🍴🚘; Walk 2; Picnics 2a and 2b), heading for the seven windmills on the horizon, one of which is still in use. Once past the windmills descend through **Peksimet**, now largely uninhabited, to **Derekoy** (where Walk 8 ends), and back to the main road where you turn left towards Bodrum. Approaching Ortakent from this angle

Car tour 7: Rock tombs on the river trip from Dalyan to Caunos (see the notes beside the photograph on page 22 for more information about this interesting river trip). You can get to Dalyan by boat (5h) or dolmus from Marmaris, as well as by car — use the Fethiye dolmus, but transfer at Ortaca to the the local dolmus.

Car tour 10: Views over the Gulf of Gokova, en route to Sedir Adasi.

affords an excellent view of the windmills, in serried rank up the bare hillside. Just through **Ortakent** turn left (42.9km), to climb up the side of a valley towards yet more windmills gracing the skyline. Pass the Yaka track (45.1km) on the left, an alternative end to Walks 4 and 5, before reaching the Dagbelen track on the right (48km; Walks 6 and 7; Picnic 6). A fantastic panorama (📷) greets you on rising over the hill, the start of a winding descent towards the olive and tangerine groves which cover the plain below.

Pass the trail to Sandima off left in 49.3km (Walk 5; Picnics 3b and 5), and then the road to Gundogan off right (51.3km), before you come into **Yalikavak** in 53km (Walks 3 and 4; Picnics 3a, 3b; photograph page 63). Park in the square as you enter or, preferably, down the road on the left, just past and down by the side of the mosque. When you leave Yalikavak, the junction to Gundogan is soon reached (54.5km); turn left onto it. You will be fascinated on the approach to **Gokcebel** (55km) by the unusual rock formations. Keep along the main road; inland Gundogan is seen nestling below high rocks to the left. After 60.1km the trail to Dagbelen (where Walk 7 and Picnics 6 and 7 start) is passed on the right, before the road sweeps up and over to crest the hill.

There is a distinct softening of the landscape now, as pine-clad hills replace the previous craggy terrain. After passing the old village of Yukari Golkoy on the right, you reach a surfaced road off left to Turkbuku and Golkoy (62.1km). (A detour here would take you past some rock tombs and through the villages, adding 8km to your overall total. You would rejoin the main road further along, at the 64km-point in the tour.) If you are observant, you might spot amongst the pines along this stretch of road the traditional tents of the *Yoruks* (nomads) blending unobtrusively into their surroundings (although they usually retreat to the cool of the mountains in summer). Keep an eye on the road here for furrows, potholes, and wandering cattle. Good coastal views (📷) can be enjoyed on the approach to **Torba** (72.6km), after which you soon reach the main Milas-to-Bodrum road junction (74.7km), where you at first turn right towards Bodrum. However, be ready to turn left to Mumcular at the top of the hill (77.2km).

This is the scenic winding old road to Milas. Keep up left at the fork right to Yaliciftlik (81.3km) and again when a surfaced road goes right to Kizilagac (82.5km). Here you encounter an area of cultivation before plunging back into the pine woods. After the next fork (85.1km), where you keep up left, well-maintained olive groves and extensive cultivation (ploughed by oxen), herald the approach of habitation. Camlik is indicated down a surfaced road left (93.1km), but continue ahead to a shady forested area on the right (94.7km) — an ideal refreshment stop.

Pine forests are left behind as you head down onto a plain, passing a timber collection area on the left, before going through **Pinarlibelen** after 102.4km. Suddenly new vistas unfold as you leave the winding woodland road to cross the plain. Villages are dotted all around, and it's not an unusual sight to see camels and donkeys grazing together. The small country town of **Mumcular** (formerly Karaova; 110km ♣🍴WC) is reached; Bodrum's new airport is under construction near here. Soon turn right to **Comlekci** (117.8km); park in or near the square. In no time at all you'll be enticed to the carpets and a glass of *cay*. The villagers work together in a co-operative, and it is possible to see the various processes involved in the production of 'Milas' carpets, so allow yourself enough time. Other villages in the area also work in this way.

Return to the main road and turn right (120.7km). On reaching **Dorttepe** (124km), look carefully for a left turn onto a narrow surfaced road, which winds through pleasant countryside, finally heading down through the pines to join the Milas/Bodrum road on the outskirts of **Guvercinlik** (130.9km ♣🏠🔺⚔🍴⚓). Turn left, back towards Bodrum. Pine-clad hills edge the road, and islands set in an ultramarine sea provide the views, as you sweep along the coastline, before turning inland to cross the peninsula. Turn left (150.8) to return to Bodrum centre.

Bodrum • Heraklia • Priene • Miletus • Euromos • Bodrum

297.5km/186mi; about 4 hours 30min driving. Exit Bodrum from the main mosque (see town plan on the touring map).

On route: Walk 11

Good surfaced roads, with the occasional rough patch, and a fairly good stabilised track from the main road to Heraklia

At first glance you may be tempted to label this tour an historian's indulgence, but there are plenty of visual delights in store as well. Even if old rocks aren't your forte, you'll certainly be mesmerised by Heraklia, at the foot of ancient Mount Latmos (now Besparmak Dagi; 1500m), by the shores of Lake Bafa ('Bafa Golu'). Priene and Miletus, now high and dry, were once lapped by the sea. This tour is truly a remarkable journey into the past.

Head out of Bodrum past the bus station, turning right on meeting the ring road towards Milas. Keep on the main road as it crosses the peninsula and then follows the coastline to **Guvercinlik** (20.5 ▲▲▲△✕☞♦). The road is good, but beware of some tight bends. From here the route sweeps over hills and across cotton-growing plains ringed by hills, where villages fit snugly onto the slopes, surrounded by olive groves. Pass through **Koru** (38.5km), a straggly village, before rising up through a rocky cutting — close to the siting of ancient Cindya to the right — and then descending onto the Milas plain.

Turn left after 47.8km, following signs for Izmir and Milas. You're soon on the dual carriageway which skirts Milas. Ignore the left turns into Milas at 49.1km and 52.2km (where the dual carriageway ends). Note the signposted road off to the right at this point — to Labranda (**π**; Walk 11). The bus station is passed on the left (53km), after which the road narrows and the terrain becomes more barren. Your route now undulates between hills — some

Car tour 2: Bafa Island is connected to the mainland by a causeway. The ruined Byzantine monastery on the island is a relic from the middle ages, when Christians sought refuge in remote locations from persecution.

20

clad in olive trees, others stark and bare —, intimate valley floors, and cotton fields. Look for the ancient bridge on the right and part of the old road as you cross a modern bridge in 57.8km. You'll also spot a sign to Iassos (**⛩**) at 61.4km (18km down the road on the left) and another at 64km, pointing the way right to Euromos (**⛩**). As you pass through **Selimiye** (67km ⊕) the mountains become more dominant, with green-cloaked rolling hills at their feet. Olive groves surround **Ekindere** (71.4km), and interesting vertical rock formations can be seen to the right. There is now a definite mountain air as you negotiate a tunnel (76km). The tunnel is short, but a bend in the centre impedes vision, so reduce speed.

Reach **Canici** (79.7km ✕⊕), where the familiar yellow sign points us right to Kalikiri and Heraklia (10km away). Turn right onto the wide stabilised track. There are glimpses of Lake Bafa over left as you drive past tall elegant poplars (*Populus alba*). After 84.4km there is a superb view ahead (📷) of Bucak village, built onto the rocks, as the landscape becomes more forbidding and hostile. Here is incredible scenery with fantastic rock shapes, reminiscent of Selge in Antalya, as though some giant hand has built a huge fortress of its own. Evidence of ruins all around announce your approach to Heraklia. A track down left (87.4km), just as you reach Heraklia, leads to the restaurants and shore, where there is a fine shingle

beach, a good picnic spot. Park by the shore or at the entrance to the village of **Kalikiri**. The view of the village built around part of Heraklia is an impressive sight from the shore; to enjoy it more fully, go early or late during the summer months, leaving plenty of time for exploration.

Heraklia ★(ᴨ✕) is a place to linger but, when you can tear yourself away, return by the same route to the main road (97.4km) and turn right. The countryside is softened by olive groves, and Heraklia can be seen across the lake on the approach to **Pinarcik** (100.6km). As you pass a 'Bafa Golu' ('Lake Bafa') sign in 104.2km, you will see the island shown on page 20, with its ruined Byzantine monastery. Leave the lake after driving along a narrow surfaced road above the shore, and head for a gap in the macchie-covered hills. Crest the brow of the hill and head down onto an extensive plain, passing a road off left (121.2km) signposted Miletus (also called Milet; ᴨ) and Didim (ᴨ). Cross the Menderes river, the boundary between the ancient kingdoms of Ionia and Caria. Silt deposited by this river created the massive plain of today, where there was once sea — and isolated Lake Bafa in the process. The elevated road leads directly across the plain through cultivation and scattered farmsteads; the countryside becomes more green as you near the mountains on the left.

Car tour 7: The boat trip from Dalyan to Caunos is a delightful, unusual and interesting trip. You sail between reed beds down-river to the sea, with an abundance of bird life and terrapins to observe. If you fancy a mud bath, the trip can include a visit up-river, back past Dalyan, to some sulphur springs and the lake. Look out, too, for the Loggerhead turtles in the river in summer. See also photograph on page 17.

The front row of the theatre at Priene is remarkably well preserved, with five thrones of honour spaced around the orchestra. It is believed that these special seats were reserved for the priests.

Turn left at the boundary of Soke (145.9km), following signs for Priene and Milet. The road now runs along the base of the bare mountains up on the right. Reach **Gullubahce** (152.9km ✕⛽), where you encounter dual carriageway. Be ready to fork right in 155.7km, onto another stretch of dual carriageway leading to Priene (straight on would take you to Miletus). A signpost at 156.3km points you right to **Priene★** (Π), a wonderful site, where the beautiful and intimate theatre is well preserved. Retrace your route back to the main road, keeping right in the one-way system in the village (WC) below the site. Rejoin the dual carriageway, then turn right for Miletus on meeting the main road (157.4km). Notice the interesting castle over to the right at **Atburgazi** (163.4km). Take the road left signposted Milet and Didim (166.6km), swinging away from the mountains now and heading back across the plain. Miletus is in view ahead to the left for a time, before you reach the left turn to it. The road leads directly onto the site, **Milet★** (179.6km Π✕WC), where the most striking feature is the theatre.

To continue, return to the main road and turn left, passing through the village of **Balat** and heading towards the tree-clad rolling hills which edge the plain. **Akkoy** is reached in 185.7km; here you turn left back to Lake Bafa (signposted 'Milas' and 'Izmir'). (At this point, if you are particularly keen on ancient sites, you could continue ahead to Didim (15km Π) and a further 3km to the sandy beach at Altinkum; these are not included in our tour.) Having turned left, views of Miletus can be enjoyed as you drive along, skimming the foothills bordering the plain.

Meet the main Milas-to-Soke road in 192.6km and turn right for Bodrum. You are now retracing your original route. Enjoy magnificent views across Lake Bafa, where you can clearly see Heraklia, strategically positioned at the base of towering and forbidding mountains. After passing through **Selimiye** (232.9km), turn left to **Euromos** (Π), situated near the main road. From this site return to Bodrum, taking extra care on the Milas by-pass at the end of the dual carriageway, as traffic coming in from the right may not stop. Take care also at the small roundabout very soon afterwards, where the right of way is questionable.

Bodrum • Temple of Lagina • Cine Cayi Gorge • Alabanda • Alinda • Bodrum

325km/203mi; about 5 hours driving. Exit Bodrum from the main mosque (see town plan on the touring map).

En route: ⊼ at Tuzabat; short walk to the Temple of Lagina

Good surfaced roads throughout, with occasional rough patches, mainly between Cine and Alinda via Alabanda. A word of warning — don't be tempted by possible short cuts along the tracks shown on some maps; they either don't exist or are unfit for most vehicles.

Travel deeper into ancient Caria to enjoy magnificent vistas and visit more remote, and thus less frequented, sites of interest. Explore Turkish villages built in and around cities of antiquity, and marvel at a spectacular ancient cobbled bridge spanning a scenic gorge.

Leave Bodrum using the notes for Car tour 2 as far as the 47.8km point. Instead of turning left to Milas, keep ahead towards Yatagan and Mugla. You are now heading towards the mountains, across the plain where vines are grown. As you start into a long picturesque climb through pines and macchie, there are good views (📷) back across the plain to Milas. Having climbed up into the mountains, the road passes through the village of **Tuzabat** (58.3km 📷), with its photogenic farms, before reaching a picnic area on the right (60.7km ⊼). Your curiosity might be aroused by the striking *'terra rossa'* — weathered limestone which produces a rich red soil and is a feature of this area. After passing through **Karalti** (70.2km), where we saw a tobacco market in progress, the road starts to descend through **Eskihisar** (73.4km).

There is a dramatic change now, as the landscape becomes more of a moonscape, the culprit being a huge quarry on the left which dominates the scenery for a time. Yatagan can be seen ahead as you turn left in 80.7km, alongside the power station on the left, to Turgut and Lagina. Once past the power station, you're back in pleasant countryside, driving along the edge of a saucer-shaped plain on the right. You cross the boundary of Turgut in 88.7km. Assuming that you will want to walk to the **Temple of Lagina ★ (🏛)** on your own*, turn right 0.4km later, to park almost immediately — near an old trail off to the left. The pleasant 10min short walk described below

*If you want a guide to take you to the site, carry on into Turgut's main square and just mention 'Lagina'; someone will soon find the curator for you. Take him in the car with you back to the start of the trail and return him to Turgut afterwards. There was no entry charge when we went, but the current policy is to introduce charges, even for the smaller sites. This diversion adds 4km to your overall total.

takes you through olive groves to the site; what little remains of it sits above the plain in an idyllic setting.

Short walk: Go down the trail for two minutes, and then down a path on the right for another two minutes, before following another path through a wall on the right. Follow this path diagonally through the olive grove, to emerge on a corner. Your route is ahead, but a brief foray to the right leads to a spring which was once part of the site. Back at the corner, continue down the path, with a wall on your left and, at a path junction just before a ruined building, turn right. Turn right again at the next junction, along the side of a field. As you descend, the ruins are visible to your left, and the path takes you left into the field and to Lagina.

Return to the main Yatagan road and turn left (97.5km), reaching the Mugla/Izmir road in 102.1km, where you again turn left. The countryside is momentarily mellowed by pines, olives and poplars, before a dramatic change at the start of the **Cine Cayi Gorge ★**. Reminiscent of Heraklia (Car tour 2), which is actually on a line over to the left, the same giant hand has again fashioned a hostile yet impelling landscape. After passing a large parking area on the right (117.7km) keep a sharp eye open for the bridge across the gorge (120.5km). Pull off the road to park, and walk across this marvellous ancient narrow bridge (★ 📷) with its four arches, before continuing through the gorge and down onto the plain.

When you reach **Cine** (138.9km ▲✕🖃⊕♨), watch out for the yellow sign in the centre, indicating a left turn to Alabanda. It's easily missed, so be prepared to turn left in 140.5km, into a narrow street. Beware of sleeping policemen and a big dip in the paved road. At a fork in 0.5km, go left and follow another sign to Alabanda (just beyond a mosque), sending you round to the right (yet another

Car tour 7 and Walk 22: It's worth a detour into Akcapinar just to admire this 3km-long tunnel of eucalyptus trees, which runs straight as a die across the plain.

At Marmaris.
Left: Ataturk Parki
(see notes on
page 40).
Below: the setting
for Picnic 23 —
a lovely glade,
by a ruined mill
and a pool.

sleeping policeman). Park by the roadside at **Alabanda** ★ (148km **⊓**). There are some ruins on the right, but most are in and around the village up to the left. Leave Alabanda along the road climbing into the mountains — a very scenic drive through small Turkish villages, some of them, like **Guney** (160.8km), with very old houses.

On reaching a T-junction (169km) turn right to Karpuzlu. (By the way, don't expect to see a lake north of Karpuzlu, even though it is shown on some maps; it no longer exists.) The ruins of Alinda are now clearly visible above the village. In **Karpuzlu** (169.4km) turn right into the centre and park by the roadside. This is a friendly village and, if things aren't too busy, you'll possibly be offered tea and a guide. To find an old trail up into the ruins of **Alinda** ★ (**⊓**), retrace a few steps — to where you turned right into the centre. Turn up right here and, almost immediately, you'll see a trail up right on the corner ahead. From here choose your own route to this fascinating and natural site. To leave Alinda, continue through the town along the main street and head for Cine along a good, surfaced road. In no time at all, the road leads you through sparsely-covered rolling hills and past flat pockets of cultivation, to the main Mugla/Izmir road (194.8km). Turn right, back into **Cine**, where you turned off to Alabanda (201.4km). From here, follow the outward route (in reverse, from the 140.5km-point) directly back to Bodrum.

4 EPHESUS FROM BODRUM
Bodrum • Soke • Selcuk • Ephesus • Bodrum

352.4km/220mi; about 6 hours driving over 2 days (or, as a 1-day return trip to Ephesus: the same distance and driving time). Exit Bodrum from the main mosque (see town plan on the touring map).

On route: Walk 11

Ephesus is one of the major ancient sites and well worth a visit. The drive from Bodrum is fairly straightforward, through interesting countryside, and with no large towns to negotiate. Given an early start, one day should be sufficient for a quick visit to the site, Mary's house and the excellent museum in Selcuk. Two days would allow for more relaxed exploration and a possible look at Kusadasi. There is plenty of accommodation available in Selcuk but, if you intend to stay overnight, secure a room on arrival — especially in high season. The tourist information office opposite the museum in Selcuk will provide you with all local information. Guided tours are also available and are usually excellent, the main drawback being the obligatory diversion into a local carpet establishment afterwards. A visit to a carpet shop in Turkey is a must and very enjoyable as long as it isn't too protracted — which is often the case on organised tours. The surfaced roads are, on the whole, good, with only the occasional rough patch encountered.

Use the notes for Tour 2 as far as the boundary of Soke, omitting the diversion to Heraklia. Keep straight along the main road into **Soke** (133.2km ♦✕✖⊕WC) and continue through it, heading for the main Aydin/Izmir road at Ortaklar. Don't follow signs to Kusadasi. Just before reaching Ortaklar you drive through the site of ancient Magnesia. At **Ortaklar** (154.2km) turn left for Izmir and Selcuk. You may be surprised to see a railway line alongside the road here. Railways don't penetrate further south than this point, and no new ones have been built since the days of Ataturk.

The countryside is more undulating and interesting before you reach **Camlik**, but becomes barren again as you descend to **Selcuk** ★ (176.2km ♦▲▲ ▲△✕✖⊕MWC). At the main crossroads, just before the bus station, turn left and you'll find a tourist information office on the right, near the museum. **Ephesus** ★ (𝕀𝕋) lies a further 3km along this road; turn left to the site just beyond the Tusan Motel. Mary's house ('Meryemana'), above Ephesus, is where the Virgin Mary is believed to have spent the last days of her life.

Return to Bodrum by the same route or, if you are staying in Kusadasi, make for Soke and then Kusadasi.

 Long-distance travel in Turkey is both very cheap and comfortable. It is easy to plan your own trip to Ephesus using the coach service from Bodrum or Marmaris to Izmir (see timetable section). The bus drops you off outside the bus station in Selcuk, where you can catch a local *dolmus* to the site entrance. It is a long day, so be prepared to stay overnight in Selcuk, where there is plenty of accommodation.

5 . PAMUKKALE ('COTTON CASTLE') FROM BODRUM

Bodrum • Yatagan • Mugla by-pass • Denizli • Pamukkale • Aphrodisias • Nyssa • Aydin • Bodrum

630km/394mi; about nine hours driving over 2 days (or, as a 1-day return trip to Pamukkale alone: 543km/339mi; about 8 hours driving). Exit Bodrum from the main mosque (see town plan on touring map).

En route: ☐ at Camlica and Dandalaz

Generally good road surfaces, but with a few rough sections. An 18km-long stretch of unfinished road, beginning at around the 133km-point, can be very dusty in summer. See also hint at the bottom of page 39.

Here is an opportunity to marvel at the spectacular panorama of the Turkish hinterland, where the plains, snow-capped mountains, and pockets of pastoral beauty paint a landscape of myriad colours and textures. Admire the brilliant white 'cotton castles' at Pamukkale; explore ancient Hierapolis, which sits higher up. Be enthralled by Aphrodisias, where much remains intact; then relax in the quiet ambience of Nyssa, where the ruins are softened by protective olive groves.

Follow the notes for Car tour 3 from Bodrum to **Yatagan**, ignoring the diversion to Turgut. On reaching the main Mugla/Izmir road (85.3km) turn right towards Mugla. Continue along this road, but be ready for a right turn onto the **Mugla by-pass** after 106.8km. Mugla makes a most impressive sight (🎥) as you come over the crest of a hill, but don't feast your eyes on it too long, or you might miss the right turn onto the by-pass. At the roundabout (113.1km) at the end of the by-pass, cross the Mugla/Fethiye road and continue across the plain, in the direction of Denizli.

You're now heading towards the mountains and the most scenic part of the route. If you're ready for a break, there's a picnic area set amongst pine trees on the right at **Camlica** (126.8km ☐). There is a pervasive alpine feel as you sweep up into the mountains, wending through massive rocky cuttings and past red-roofed houses tucked into the hollows. Glimpses of distant snow-capped mountains add to the delight of the ever-changing

Aphrodisias is a truly magnificent site with its own museum, excellent theatre and stadium. The odeon, shown here, is where the elders met in council.

panorama. The constant wonder of Turkey's scenery will continue to surprise you. The vista before you, as you begin to descend to a plain in 150km, suddenly transports you from the Alps to the desert. In the centre of the plain, a curious hill surmounted by a vertical rock formation glows red in the sunlight, whilst waves of creamy yellow soil give the impression of sand dunes.

After **Kale** (185.9km ✖🚐) the road narrows and you now cross a large cultivated plain surrounded by hills and mountains. The outskirts of **Tavas** (🛢⊕) are reached in 211.4km; here there is a turn-off to Aphrodisias, which you ignore. Beware of traffic coming in from the left when passing the town itself, as it doesn't always stop. An amazing feature of Tavas is the number of minarets for a town of its size; we counted at least fifteen.

At a T-junction (the Acipayam/Denizli road; 227.6km), bear left. The wide modern road takes you on a spectacular mountain run before descending to Denizli. A lay-by on the right (243km 📷) enables you to stop a moment to enjoy the fantastic panorama over the plain below. You might even be able to spot the white patch on the hillside beyond and to the right of Denizli — Pamukkale. When you reach the dual carriageway, keep in the right-hand lane following the signs for Pamukkale and Afyon. Turn right at the roundabout (254.2km) for Pamukkale, before you actually reach the centre of **Denizli** (🏨🛏✖🚐➔WC), then turn left (signposted 'Pamukkale') in 258.2km. Almost immediately you'll notice the left turn to Laodica (🏛) and perhaps resolve to visit it later. Ahead is the white mass that is Pamukkale — Turkish for 'cotton castle'.

Enter the village of **Pamukkale** (271.5km 🛢🏨🛏△✖➔ 📷⊕), below the travertines ★ (the white stalactite-draped shallow bowls shown in the photograph on page 31). If you plan to stay overnight, the best course of action is to park on the right at the bottom of the village and walk into the centre on the left. This way you avoid the hordes of pension touts who wait in the car park above the travertines. In high season, when it's very busy, bargaining over pension prices is difficult — but otherwise don't hesitate. The site of **Hierapolis** ★ (🏛🏨✖➔📷MWC) lies above the travertines. We usually leave our car in the village, at our accommodation, and walk from there along a path up onto the travertines. Don't forget your sunglasses!

Leave Pamukkale by retracing the incoming route, turning left at the roundabout in Denizli (signposted to Tavas and Acipayam). Back at **Tavas** (57.5km), take care where the road forks right into the town. You keep left on the main road at this point, but traffic does tend to come out of the town without stopping. Turn right at Tavas for Aphrodisias, and then keep left at the fork 5km later. The barren but striking mountain range, prominent as you crossed the plain from Mugla, is now on the right as you travel through gently undulating countryside. At **Geyre** (95.2km) look for the sign on the left for Aphrodisias. Turn left here (95.4km) into the narrow surfaced road and park in the car park on the left 0.5km later. **Aphrodisias ★ (⛪M;** photograph page 28) is a truly magnificent site. Allow at least two hours for exploration.

Return to the main road, and turn left to continue in the direction of Izmir. Just through **Dandalaz**, there's a shaded picnic area on the left immediately after crossing a bridge (105.8km ✖🏕️🌳). It's worth a short stop to admire the gorge below the picnic site and the ancient bridge on the far side of the road. At **Karacasu**, where you meet cross-roads (108.6km), turn right. Then, almost immediately, turn right again at the roundabout (signposted 'Izmir'). Descend to the plain and look for storks nests along the tree-lined road through **Yenice** (121.1km).

When you meet the main Denizli/Izmir road (133.5km), turn left towards Aydin. Continue along this road, taking care over the large hump as you cross the railway line (149km). The juniper tree-lined road of **Sultanhisar** is reached in 163.3km, where you soon turn right, following the sign to Nyssa. Cross the railway line and head into the town centre. Another sign now directs you up into the countryside above Sultanhisar to the lovely, tranquil site of **Nyssa ★** (166.4km ⛪🚻WC). Enjoy extensive views out over the plain below from the large theatre, then follow the signs, further along the road, to the excellently-preserved council house set peacefully in the olive groves. From Nyssa return to the main road, turning right towards Aydin. If you are lucky enough to be in Turkey in April, the wonderful scent of orange blossom pervades the air where oranges are grown, and at Sultanhisar it is particularly noticeable.

On coming into **Aydin** (194.8km ⛽🏨🛏️✖🚌🏪⊕WC), turn left (signposted for Dalaman Airport, Marmaris, Cine and Mugla) at the second set of traffic lights (197.9km), which is also a roundabout. (A disconcerting point here is that you can't see the signpost until you reach the far side of the roundabout, so position yourself in the outside lane ready to turn left.) Travel across the plain towards the hills, which you pass through, then swing right to cross yet another plain to **Cine** (227.4km ⛪▲✕⛽⊕). From here return to Bodrum via the Cine Cayi Gorge, Yatagan and Milas (Car tour 3 describes the route, but in reverse).

The travertines at Pamukkale rise in turrets to the plateau 120m above, looking like something out of a fairy tale. They have been formed by calcium-rich water, fed from thermal springs in the mountains behind, cascading gently down the hillside over the centuries. Hierapolis was built here because of the thermal springs, and people still come to bathe in the warm waters (Car tours 5 and 10).

6 THE SERPENTINE RUN

Marmaris • Datca • Knidos • Marmaris

217.6km/136mi; about 6 hours driving. Exit Marmaris from the Ataturk statue (see town plan and area enlargement on the touring map).

On route: Picnics (see pages 9-12) 13, 14, 18; Walks 13, 14, 15, 18, 19

Well surfaced but narrow road to Datca. From there we follow another surfaced road for 7km, before the route reverts to a stabilised track (rough for the final 7km). The stabilised track is manageable by car in dry conditions, but a jeep is preferable. Note that the only petrol station on the peninsula is at Datca. A new track was being made just beyond the point where the surfaced road ended en route to Knidos but, as far as we can tell, it shouldn't affect our directions.

A breathtaking run along the Datca Peninsula to its tip and the remains of Knidos, this is not a tour for the faint-hearted, but is certainly spellbinding. Awesome views, a picturesque fishing village, and an ancient outpost provide the ingredients for an unforgettable day.

Leave Marmaris from the Ataturk statue, heading in the direction of the harbour. Turn left to pass the post office, then left again at the T-junction on the road to Mugla. The Datca road is reached after 0.6km; turn left to Datca. Cross the plain of Marmaris before beginning the ascent up into the hills at **Armutalan** (2.5km; Walks 13, 14, 15; Picnics 13 and 14). A vantage point on the left (4.9km 📷) provides a good view over the plain back to Marmaris as you ascend through pines. The horseshoe bend over a bridge (8.3km) is the point where Walks 13 and 14 emerge.

Descend to cross another plain, past a eucalyptus plantation, and through **Degirmenyani** (16.1km ✕), where you might spot storks. A left turn to Hisaronu and Orhaniye is passed in 19.1km (Walk 18 and Picnic 18).

Two lovely harbours at Knidos attract the yachting fraternity in summer.

You are soon heading back into the hills again, past unusual rock conglomerate. If it is convenient, as you come over the pass in 36.4km, pull off the road to the right, as the panoramas are quite spectacular (📷). As you descend, a fountain on the left (41.4km) provides a shaded area for a rest. Back down at sea level, serpentine rock (see Walk 15) gives way to limestone and cultivation. In spring, chrysanthemums line the road, and the fields are a mass of striking-red poppies. The right turn to Knidos is passed in 70.7km, soon after entering **Resadiye**; but first continue ahead. Some 0.8km later, the road appears to fork: keep left and in 75.1km park in the car park on your left, opposite the bus station in **Datca** ★ (74km ⅃▲▲▲△ ✗🏠🚉⊕📷WC; Walk 19; photograph page 116).

When you are ready to leave Datca, return to where you turn left to Knidos (79.6km) and keep left at a fork in 80.2km. The surfaced road is now heading into more wild and mountainous country, becoming a stabilised track after 86km. At the signpost to Knidos keep round to the right, not down left. But keep left at the fork in 91.1km and start to descend. Go right at the fork in 93.3km. Notice some interesting rock formations and small caves over right as you pass through a small hamlet and descend to the valley bottom. Keep right (96.9km) where a track goes off left, and then go left at a fork (97.1km). The track becomes very narrow through the next hamlet, after which you swing right for Knidos (98.9km).

Enter the village of **Yaka** (100.1km), keeping round to the right as a track enters from the left (100.8km). Can you spot some old windmills in the vicinity, especially on the right as you enter **Cumali** (103.2km)? Turn right opposite the mosque in the centre of Cumali. Keep right at the fork in 104.2km, and go straight ahead almost immediately, where a track forks off right. At **Yazakoy** (105.3km) the track goes round to the left in the village. Continue down to the right at the fork in 106.2km, which is also the start of the rough section of track. Scattered remains, mainly walling, herald the proximity of Knidos, as you drive along a ledge of the cliff on what is now fairly rough track, with good views of the sea down left (📷).

On arrival at **Knidos** ★ (113.6km ��✗; photograph opposite), park on the grass verge to the left. The custodian will appear to collect your entrance fee, to offer information, and to act as a guide — should you require one.

Return along the same route, bearing *right* towards Datca in 128.4km, to rejoin your original route.

7 KING CAUNOS AND CLEOPATRA

Marmaris • Dalyan • Sedir Adasi • Marmaris

184.8km/115.5mi; about 3 hours 50 min driving. Exit Marmaris from the Ataturk statue (see town plan on the touring map).

On route: Picnics (see pages 9-12): 12a, 12b, 20, 21, 23; Walks 12, 20-23.

With only a few exceptions, the main roads are quite good. The old road between the eucalyptus trees at Akcapinar requires your attention, and watch for bad potholes between Yuvarlakcay and Dalyan. A new road alongside the eucalyptus tunnel, by-passing Akcapinar, might now be fully in use. We suggest driving straight to Dalyan before it becomes too busy, then visiting Sedir Adasi on your return, for a swim. If you have more time, spend a full day at each location. A word of warning: Cleopatra's beach on Sedir Adasi is beautiful, but it isn't really safe for young children and non-swimmers, as the sea bed shelves steeply.

Multifarious shades of fresh green, and poppies dancing by the roadside provide the colour ... a tunnel of eucalyptus trees offers welcome shade ... the city of mythical King Caunos, and Cleopatra's intimate beach, give the fascination and delight to this tour.

Leave Marmaris from the Ataturk statue, as in Tour 6 but, when you reach the Datca road (0.6km) continue ahead in the direction of Mugla. Note the Beldibi fork to the left after 1.2km (Walks 12 and 15; Picnics 12a and b). Keep ahead up the valley, when the by-pass road joins from the right (1.6km; Walk 23; Picnic 23). Enjoy a scenic run up the wooded hillside of the Beldibi valley (📷 at 3.4km). Marmaris is lost from view as you rise over the crest, to descend between green-clad hills. Pass the turning left to Sedir Adasi (12.5km). In 13.9km, there is a signposted left turn to Camlikoyu ('Camli village'); both short versions of Walk 20 end here. The next four landmarks are all on the left, starting as you cross the bridge into Cetibeli: a trout restaurant at 16.9km (Walk 20 and Picnic 20); a new mosque (17.5km; Walk 21 and Picnic 21); a track where Alternative walk 21 ends (17.8km); and, finally, where the road heads back up into pines, another track, where the main route of Walk 21 ends (20.2km).

Descend to **Gokce** (23.2km ⏷✖), where Walk 22 ends; then swing right into **Akcapinar** (✖; Walk 22; photograph page 25) in 24.5km. (Ignore the new road straight ahead at this point.) At the main Fethiye/Izmir junction (28km ✖⛽), turn right to Fethiye. If you scan the wetlands to your right, you may be lucky enough to see the storks common to this area. Keep on this road, passing through hamlets and crossing plains surrounded by pine woods and mountains. The lake close to Dalyan comes into view after **Toparlar** (56.2km) and is much closer when you reach

34

Koycegiz (59.5km). Be ready to turn right into a minor surfaced road signposted to Dalyan and Caunos immediately after crossing the river at **Yuvarlakcay** (69km ✕). (Reduce speed as the road has many potholes.) Keep right at the fork in **Tepearasi** (74.9km), and then bear right again in 76.7km. At a crossroads (81.3km), keep ahead on a good road into Dalyan. (A left turn here goes to Ortaca and Fethiye — an alternative route for our return. The unfinished road to the left will eventually go to Koycegiz.)

Arriving in **Dalyan** ★ (82.7km ♨▲▲✕⬛🖃⊕🖾 WC), keep round to the right, towards the river, and park on the left near the mosque. The office for the boat trip to **Caunos** ★ (**ⅱ🖾**WC; described in the notes beside the photographs on pages 17 and 24) is a wooden hut on the riverside past the mosque. Look at the map on the outside, decide what you want to see, then ask the charge to hire a boat (allow at least three hours for the trip). It's possible to negotiate a price when it's not too busy. The entrance fee to the site is not included in the cost of the boat trip. Mythical King Caunos was purportedly an invention of the early inhabitants of Caunos, to give them an identity.

To return, we bear right towards Fethiye at the crossroads (84km). At the roundabout in **Ortaca** (94.6km ♨▲▲✕⊕WC) turn left, shortly to rejoin the main Fethiye/Izmir road, where you again turn left towards Izmir. Follow your outgoing route past Camli and, when you reach the road to Sedir Adasi (152.9km), turn right and head down a pleasant cultivated valley towards the sea. There is a WC on the left (158.5km) just before you reach the shore, from where boats will also take you to Sedir Adasi in summer. Follow the road up to the left, where there are good views over the Gulf of Gokova (🖾; photograph page 18). As you descend, turn right (162km) onto a track leading to the 'Sedir Motel'. Keep right at the first fork, left at the next, and then right again. Enquire at the motel (162.6km) about a boat to take you the very short distance to **Sedir Adasi** ★ ('Cedar Island').* On the eastern side of the island lie the remains of the once-important ancient city of Cedreae, including a theatre, but beware of unprotected holes as you scramble around. It is believed that the white sand at **Cleopatra's beach** ★ was shipped from the Red Sea to the island especially for her.

The return to Marmaris is along the same route.

*They operate even out of season. There is a charge to go onto the island in the season, when a buffet, showers and toilets are available at the beach. Arrange with the boatman to return for you — or to wait.

8 LYCIAN ADVENTURE

Marmaris • Fethiye (Telmessus) • Letoon • Kalkan • Xanthos • Patara • Marmaris

448km/280mi; about 8 hours driving. Exit Marmaris from the Ataturk statue (see town plan on the touring map).

On route: Picnics (see pages 9-12) 12a, 12b, 20, 21, 23; Walks 12, 20-23.

This is a two-day tour (overnight at Kalkan). For a one-day trip to Fethiye, there would be ample time to visit the much-photographed beauty spot of Olu Deniz, and for swimming: from the 132.2km-point go direct to Olu Deniz (12km). Surfaced roads throughout, the only exception being the diversion to Patara, which is along a stabilised track and very dusty in summer. In the height of summer, historical sites are best visited as early or late in the day as possible, as it can become unbearably hot.

Splendid pine forests and a plethora of ancient sites and remains add a richness to the landscape. This area is one of the most scenically beautiful in Turkey, as you cross the ancient boundary between Caria and Lycia.

From Marmaris follow the notes for Tour 7, until you reach **Yuvarlakcay** (69km). Continue along the main road and, as you by-pass Ortaca, take care on meeting a short stretch of dual carriageway on a bend (77.6km). The main route from Dalyan to Fethiye joins here, and it isn't wise to assume an automatic right of way. Again, care is needed at a roundabout on 81.7km, the turn-off to Dalaman, where you keep straight ahead on the main road. From this point, the road starts to leave the plain and rises up into the pine forest before making a spectacular descent, snaking down into a deep-sided wooded valley. The boundary between ancient Caria and Lycia lay in this region, where you now travel through pine forests and charming villages in cultivated valleys. Just before **Inlice** (105km) there is an interesting rock tomb up to the left, better viewed on the return. This area is the site of ancient Daedala, but the actual ruins — in the hills to the left — are not easily accessible.

Descend onto the green and fertile plain of Fethiye, ringed by mountains, following the line of the coast to the far side. Drive through small villages and past orange groves, until you reach a roundabout after 132.2km. The road ahead leads to Olu Deniz ★ (the 'dead sea'; so-called because it is almost land-locked), but turn right to the seafront and **Fethiye** ★ (133.5km ↨┰▲▲✕ ☞♥⊕🚗MWC). This is the site of ancient **Telmessus**, where you can see some of the finest specimens of old Lycian tombs ★.

Leave Fethiye and return to the roundabout on the main road (135km), where you keep straight ahead towards Kas and Antalya. Drive inland, towards the mountains, passing eucalyptus plantations and villages.

36

Be prepared to swing right with the main road after 156.5km (straight would take you into Kemer). Almost immediately, keep ahead for 'Kas/Antalya', when the road forks left to 'Antalya/Korkuteli'. Travellers to Antalya* should decide at this point whether or not to take the slow coastal route through Kas or the faster inland route. Lofty mountains form a barrier into the interior, as you drive south through pine forests and farmland.

A right turn to Pinara ★ (**Ⓣ**) is passed in 177.3km. (The site is not easily accessible by car; the final 2.5km is on a very rough track up a hillside, only manageable in a jeep. If you wish to visit it, park about 3.5km along the surfaced road, near the start of the track, and walk from there.) As you draw closer to the macchie-covered hills, turn right at 193.8km for Letoon. Then bear left at a T-junction and immediately right to arrive at **Letoon** ★ (198.2km **Ⓣ**), the sanctuary of Leto and her children Apollo and Artemis. A part of the foundations is now below the water table and has become a fascinating aquarium, the habitat of terrapins and water snakes. There is also a theatre to inspect.

Return to the main road and turn right to continue to Kalkan, passing Xanthos (204.5km) and Patara (211km) on the way. As the road rises up from the plain beyond **Yesilkoy**, keep right at a T-junction (219.4km). **Kalkan** (222.2km ⚓🏠🛡✗🚐🚲⊕🗺WC) is approached from above and is perched at the base of a steep hillside. Turn right into the village and head down in the direction of the harbour. Park where convenient and find accommodation for the night. Kalkan is a village with character, set by its own small bay. Many of the old houses have been converted into pensions. Kas* is only a further 28km along the coast, for those who wish to explore the region.

Next day, retrace your route back to Marmaris, taking in the sites of Patara and Xanthos along the way. Take care not to miss the left turn to Fethiye and Mugla, 3.5km from Kalkan. Turn left in 11.9km for Patara; this track is very dusty in summer. Now buried in saned dunes, the harbour at **Patara** ★ (16.2km **Ⓣ**) was once the most important in Lycia. Go back to the main road and turn left (22.4km) to continue, turning right to Xanthos opposite the mosque in **Kinik** (28.9). At **Xanthos** ★ (29.5km **Ⓣ**), park in the car park on the right, across from the theatre. Xanthos is an interesting and extensive site; its position gives it a quite romantic appeal.

On leaving Xanthos return via Fethiye to Marmaris.

*See *Landscapes of Turkey (around Antalya)*

**Marmaris • Aydin • Selcuk • Ephesus • Priene • Miletus
• Heraklia • Euromos • Milas • Yatagan • Marmaris**

*490km/306mi; about 7 hours 30 min driving over 2 days. Alternatively,
this can be a 1-day, partly circular return trip to Ephesus alone
(448km/280mi; about 6 hours 50 min driving), or a 1-day return trip via
Aydin (406km/254mi; about 6 hours 15 min driving). Exit Marmaris
from the Ataturk statue (see town plan on the touring map).*

On route: Picnics (see pages 9-12): 12a, 12b, 20, 21, 23; Walks 12, 20-
23.

*It is possible to make the trip in one day if you start early. The most direct
route is via Aydin returning the same way. But for a change of scene, try
the return route via Milas, omitting the four sites. This adds a further
42km. The road surfaces are quite good, but watch for the occasional
bumpy stretch, especially just beyond Aydin. Heraklia is reached along
stabilised track from the main road.*

A marvellous circuit encompassing the scenic Cine
Cayi gorge, magnificent Ephesus, and wild Lake
Bafa. Use the notes for Tour 7, until you meet the main
Fethiye-to-Izmir junction (28km); here turn left to 'Mugla/
Izmir'. (The sign '*Tirmanma Seridi*', as you begin a long
climb up the hillside, means 'climbing lane'.) A wonderful
panorama unfolds as you climb, the unbroken line of the
eucalyptus tunnel at Akcapinar (Car tour 7; Walk 22;
photograph page 25) being seen clearly, cutting across the
plain below. The restaurant and tourist information centre
on the left (34.7km ✕⊡) is an ideal vantage point for
admiring the views down the Gulf of Gokova ★ and over
the sea of pine-clad hills surrounding the plain. At the top
of the hill you start to descend and cross a high level plain,
before rising again between barren rolling hills. A startling
view across to Mugla sheltered below the mountains
greets you, as you crest the rise and begin the descent.

Down on the plain, at the roundabout (51.2km), turn
left onto the Mugla by-pass, then left again on meeting the
Mugla/Yatagan road (57.3km). Continue on this road, past
the junction left into Yatagan (79km). Now refer to the
notes for Car tour 3, from the 102.1km point (page 25),
and follow these to **Cine** (117.5km ⌀▲✕⊒⊕). Keep on the
main road from Cine to the roundabout in **Aydin** (153.6km
⌀▲▲▲✕⊒⊡⊕wc).(Car tour 5 follows this section, the
other way around.) Turn left at the roundabout in Aydin,
towards Izmir, immediately passing the bus station on the
right. Follow the Izmir road (bumpy in places) for the final
49km to **Selcuk**. Refer to the notes for Car tour 4 from
Ortaklar (the 154.2km-point, page 27), to cover the last
22km to **Selcuk** ★ (⌀▲▲▲△✕⊒⊡⊕Mwc) and for what
to do on arrival.

From Selcuk return to Ortaklar, and there bear right for Soke. Some 5km beyond the centre of **Soke** (⛽️✕🚆⊕wc), turn right for Priene, using the notes for Car tour 2 (from the 145.9km-point, at the top of page 23). (Or, if time is short, continue along the main road directly to Milas and the Bodrum/Yatagan road. Miss out the sites, and pick up the notes below at the 170.4km-point.) The notes for Car tour 2 take you via **Priene ★(🏛)** and **Milet ★(🏛✕)** back to the Milas/Soke road, where you turn right to Milas. Now drive back past Lake Bafa via **Heraklia ★(🏛✕)** and **Euromos (🏛)**; Tour 2 covers this section in reverse. When the Milas by-pass meets the Bodrum/Yatagan road (170.4km), turn left to Yatagan and Mugla. Car tour 3 (from the 47.8km-point) will set the scene, but don't divert up to Turgut; continue straight to **Yatagan** (207.9km). Then turn right at the T-junction for Mugla and Marmaris.

10 PAMUKKALE FROM MARMARIS

Marmaris • Mugla by-pass• Pamukkale • Aphrodisias • Nyssa • Aydin • Marmaris

562km/351mi; about 9 hours driving over 2 days (or, as a 1-day return trip to Pamukkale alone: 420km/262mi; about 6 hours 30min driving). Exit Marmaris from the Ataturk statue (see town plan on touring map).

On route: Picnics (see pages 9-12) 12a, 12b, 20, 21, 23; Walks 12, 20-23.

Reasonably surfaced roads for the most part. An 18km stretch of new stabilised road between Mugla and Kale can be very dusty in summer. See the introduction to Tour 5 for details.

Follow Car tour 9 from Marmaris to the **Mugla by-pass** (51.2km). Turn right for **Denizli** (🏨🏠✕🚆🅿️wc), and use the notes for Car tour 5 (from the 113.1km-point, page 29) to reach Pammukale ★ (⛽️🏠🏨⚠️△✕🚆⊕📷). Continue following these notes, as far as **Cine** (⛽️🏠✕🅿️⊕). Past Cine, follow the main road towards Yatagan (271.9km). (Cine Cayi Gorge is described in Tour 3.) A further 21.5km brings you to the **Mugla by-pass**: immediately over the brow of a hill, turn right onto the by-pass, and then bear right again on meeting the Mugla/Fethiye road. From here return to Marmaris. (The notes for Car tour 9 describe this route in reverse, from the 51.2km-point.)

A visit to Pamukkale is easily arranged, using the excellent long-distance coach service. Use the Bodrum or Marmaris service to Denizli, and then transfer to the local *dolmus*, which passes along the main road outside the bus station, for the final short hop to Pamukkale. Be prepared to stay overnight, and read notes for Car tour 5 for more details.

11 BODRUM TO MARMARIS OR MARMARIS TO BODRUM

Bodrum • Milas • Yatagan • Marmaris • Yatagan • Milas • Bodrum

329km/206mi; about 4 hours 40 min driving return journey. Exit Bodrum from the main mosque; exit Marmaris from the Ataturk statue (see town plans on the touring map).

On route: Picnics (see pages 9-12) 12a, 12b, 20-23; Walks 12, 20-23

Good surfaced roads all the way. Markets: During winter the market is held along the seafront in both resorts, but in summer they are located as shown on the town plans. Friday is market day in Marmaris; in Bodrum the market is open from Thursday lunch-time until Friday afternoon. At present, there are no car parks in either resort.

B odrum and Marmaris are completely contrasting resorts, and this tour will guide you between the two, with suggestions for short walks en route. Pick up this circular tour at either resort.

From Bodrum, use the notes for Tour 5 as far as the roundabout at the end of the Mugla by-pass (113.1km). Turn right to Marmaris and Fethiye and continue on this road for a further 23.2km. Then turn right to Marmaris at a major junction, alongside the eucalyptus tunnel shown on page 25, just after the panoramic descent onto the plain. The road winds through pine forests, approaching Marmaris down the side of a valley. To reach the sea front, take the right fork at the roundabout on the outskirts of the town; then refer to the town plan. (For more details of the route from Mugla, see Tour 9, which covers that section in reverse.)

From Marmaris, follow the notes for Tour 9 as far as the 79km point, the junction into Yatagan. Turn left to Milas and Bodrum, keeping straight ahead in 116.5km to by-pass Milas. Continue along this road to Bodrum. After crossing the peninsula, as you come parallel with the coast down left, take the first right-hand turn into the town. (For more details of the route from Yatagan, see Tour 5, which covers that section in reverse.)

After seeing Marmaris, why not stretch your legs in Ataturk Parki or try Walk 23 to the waterfalls (see photographs on page 26). Ataturk Parki is a beautiful, very green park which borders the sea about 1km east of the Marmaris bus station. Facilities include a car park, picnic tables, a children's play area, buffet and toilets. The 'special tree' of this region, the liquidambar (shown on page 96) abounds in the park, as does a fascinating spring flora of fritillaries, cyclamen and orchids.

After seeing Bodrum, you might sample part of Walk 10 (in reverse, see map page 85) or, if you have time, drive to Gumusluk inland village (20 minutes away) and try dramatic Walk 2 — a circular route.

40

✺ Walking

Bodrum and Marmaris are well know as holiday resorts, but few people realise what excellent bases they make for a walking holiday. The countryside around each offers unexpected and spectacular walking opportunities. The scenic variety is awe-inspiring in the rugged open volcanic regions near Bodrum, while the green-cloaked hills of Marmaris rolling into an azure-blue sea present images certain to stop you in your tracks. Whichever is the resort of your choice, there is more than enough walking to keep you occupied. All the ground work has been done so, straight from day one, you can be out in the countryside enjoying those all-too-short holidays. But please accept some words of caution. Use only the walks described here, and never try to get from one walk to another across uncharted terrain — even though it may look possible. Distances in mountains are very deceptive, and points that look close can sometimes take many hours of walking to bridge.

There are walks in this book for everyone. All the walks are graded, so just check the grade to see if it suits you and, if the grade of the main walk is too high, be sure to check all the shortened versions. If you are an **inexperienced walker**, or just looking for a gentler walk, then go for the walks graded as 'easy'. Look, too, at the picnic suggestions on pages 9-12; here you have a selection of particularly beautiful spots, many of which are easily reached in under an hour's walking.

Experienced walkers should be able to tackle most of the walks in this book, taking into account, of course, the season and the weather conditions. If a walk is very long, do be sure of your fitness before you attempt it. Don't attempt the more strenuous walks in high summer; do protect yourself from the sun and carry an ample supply of water and plenty of fruit with you. After each winter there is a new crop of uprooted trees, which are cleared only from the major tracks and may still be blocking the minor tracks. **Always remember that storm damage could make some of the walks described in this book unsafe.** Always err on the side of safety; if you have not reached one of our landmarks after a reasonable time, then you must return to the last 'sure' point and start again.

For the very **expert walkers**, there are no really tough walks, but it is possible to join some walks together to test your stamina and make the day more challenging.

Guides, waymarking, maps

Official **guides** are available in Turkey, but they are more concerned with mountaineering than walking, and none are needed for the walks in this book. We strongly recommend that anyone wishing to explore mountainous regions not described in this book should do so only in the company of a guide with local knowledge.

Most of our walks use well-established footpaths, trails, and tracks and are easily followed. There is very little **waymarking**, but it can be seen part-way along two or three of the walks at the moment. It is possible, as walking grows in popularity in these parts, that more may appear. To avoid any possible confusion, it is wiser to follow our directions at all times, rather than any route markings.

The **maps** in this book have been drawn up in the field, with reference to the best maps available and using an altimeter to measure the heights. Unfortunately, accurate and detailed maps are not yet available for Turkey from any source, and it still remains an area of some sensitivity. *Do not try to obtain large-scale maps* of the region from the local authorities for, at the very least, you will be faced with suspicion! The maps in this book are as accurate as we can make them with the available information and should help to guide you safely through all the walks.

What to take

If you are already in Turkey when you find this book, and you haven't any special equipment such as a rucksack and walking boots, you can still do some of the walks but, better still, buy some of the equipment you need locally. Boots, shoes, and trainers can all be bought fairly cheaply, provided you do not require a large size. Continental size 45 is the upper limit for men and 41 for women. Don't attempt any of the difficult walks without the proper gear or with brand new footwear. For each walk in the book the minimum year-round equipment is listed. Where walking boots are required there is, unfortunately, no substitute: you'll need to rely on the grip and ankle support they provide, and they are absolutely essential on some walks, where the path descends steeply over loose stones. All other walks should be made with stout shoes, preferably with thick rubber soles to grip on wet and slippery surfaces. Occasionally, where we feel the walk is suitable for trainers, they have been included as an option. You may find the following check list useful:

walking boots (which must be broken-in and comfortable)
waterproof rain gear (outside summer months)
long-sleeved shirt (sun protection)
long trousers, tight at ankles (sun and tic protection)
water bottle with water purifying tablets
universal sink plug (an absolute necessity)
two cardigans
woollen hat and gloves

spare boot laces
bandages and band aids
plastic plates, cups, etc
knives and openers
small rucksack
plastic groundsheet
anorak (zip opening)
sunglasses, sunhat
protective suncream
insect repellent
antiseptic cream
compass, whistle, torch
extra pair (long) socks
compact, folding umbrella

Please bear in mind that we have not done *every* walk in the book under *all* conditions. For this reason we have listed under 'Equipment' all the gear you *might* need, depending on the season, and we rely on your good judgement to modify it accordingly.

Where to stay

Bodrum: The resort of Bodrum itself is an excellent centre for a walking holiday — and where we actually stayed. It's the hub of the transport system in the region, so that you can get around to all parts of the peninsula very easily. It is a lively, bustling resort which has grown around a fine harbour and the Castle of St Peter. If you prefer somewhere quieter, there is plenty of choice around the peninsula. **Turgutreis** is the next largest town: it is still very Turkish and has not devoted itself to tourism as Bodrum has — making it a delightful place to stay. You should be able to do all the walks in the region from this base with equal facility. **Gumusluk** and **Yalikavak**, too, are both delightful resorts, and make good walking centres — but they are small, with limited accommodation. Both are well connected by *dolmus* to Bodrum, although the services to these villages are less frequent out of season. **Akyarlar**, in the south, is a peaceful resort, but rather isolated. The same is true for **Torba** and **Turkbuku** in the north. Their *dolmus* services only operate to Bodrum, making it difficult to get around the whole peninsula.

Marmaris: This is the best base for a walking holiday and where we actually stayed. Again, it is the centre for the local and long distance transport which makes it easy to get around. The old fishing village of Marmaris is centred on the castle and harbour, but has long since been swallowed up by the sizeable resort. If you prefer something smaller and quieter, **Icmeler**, which lies to the west, might suit you. It is well connected by *dolmus* to Marmaris, which means that you will have the opportunity to do all the walks in the area with only a little more travelling. Other smaller resorts, like **Turunc** and **Orhaniye**, delightful though they may be, are isolated and inconvenient, unless you have the use of a hire car to get around.

Weather

The kindest months for walking in this part of Turkey are those either side of summer: April, May, September and October — although early September can still be hot. The **two walking seasons, spring and autumn**, present different opportunities, but spring is the loveliest, with a freshness in the air and the flowers at their best.

By April the temperature is rising and, given average conditions, it is time to air the shorts. Sunny days are plentiful, but there can still be showers around or short unsettled periods. (Equally, temperatures can rise to 30°C and more.) May sees a steady transition towards the hotter, drier conditions of summer. As the temperatures continue to climb throughout June, the walking season ends. In high summer, walking is *not* advisable, owing to the constant dangers of heat exhaustion and dehydration.

At some time in September, a short unsettled spell brings a change and, although the fine weather usually continues well into the autumn and often to the end of the year, the temperatures fall back into the 20s°C. This autumn rain brings on a new spring: cyclamen suddenly brighten the woodlands and olive groves, the crocus are persuaded into flower, and it is a delight to walk again.

Winter rains can be heavy, but there are many fine days, and the cool, clear conditions are ideal for walking. February is the earliest month that can be considered, although March is a better choice, with the real possibility of some gently warm weather.

Things that bite or sting

Dogs are generally not much of a problem, although they may be encountered guarding sheep or goats. If you stay away from the animals, they are usually just content to bark a warning. **Snakes** are something you will have to be on your guard against. We saw very few throughout the spring months, but we are advised that there are more around in summer. Most are probably harmless but, if there are any of the viper species around, then great care is needed. Most snakes are more frightened of you and will move out of your way rapidly but, if they don't, the best advice is to move quietly out of their way. The real danger comes if you accidentally stand on one. For this reason, it is *imperative* that you do not walk in the countryside in open sandals, no matter how comfortable they are for walking. Always have your feet and ankles well covered, and it is a sensible precaution to wear your long trousers tucked into your socks. Take special care near water, when you are about to sit down, or when you choose to rest your hand, so unthinkingly, on a dry-stone wall.

Scorpions are around, too, but you are most likely to see them in the height of summer, when they are usually seeking shade— so don't leave any of your clothing on the ground. Accidentally turning over rocks or stones may expose them but, generally, they offer no serious threat, for their sting is more painful than dangerous for most people. In areas which are well forested, **ticks** can be a problem. As you brush through the woodlands they can get onto your clothes but, if you follow our advice about wearing long trousers and a long-sleeved shirt, you should be able to keep them off your skin. If they do manage to get to your skin, then it is necessary to make them withdraw before you take them off. An easy way to do this is to touch them with a solvent such as methylated spirits or petrol. **Bees** and **wasps** are around in summer, so make sure you carry the necessary creams and pills, especially if you are one of those people who are allergic to insect bites.

Wild boar are around in the mountains, but they are shy animals and you will be fortunate to see one. The only evidence we saw was the marks in the forest where they paw the ground.

Turkish for walkers

Not much English is spoken in this part of Turkey as yet, but this is changing rapidly. In the countryside a few words of Turkish will be helpful. Turkish is very logical and, once you have mastered a few of the rules, you can progress fairly quickly, especially with pronunciation. A number of the alphabet letters are unfamiliar to us, but their pronunciation is easy enough. The frequently encountered ones are as shown on the next page.*

*Turkish spellings are not used for place names in the text, lest they slow up your reading, but they *are* shown on the *maps* and in the *Index*.

Ç/ç   pronounced as **ch**, eg *çam*, meaning pine, sounds like '**ch**am'

Ş/ş   pronounced as **sh**, eg *şeker*, meaning sugar, sounds like **sh**eker

Ğ/ğ   just elongates the previous vowel, eg *dağ*, meaning mountain, sounds like **daa**.

Ö/ö   The letters with diaeresis above, ö and ü, sound exactly as in
Ü/ü   German.

If you master these, together with the fact that the ordinary letter 'C' is pronounced like 'J', then you should be able to pronounce virtually all the place names used in this book. We strongly recommend that you use an inexpensive phrase book like Berlitz or Hugo's *Turkish Phrase Book*, which not only give easily-understood pronunciation hints, but also a selection of useful phrases.

Here's one way to ask directions in Turkish and understand the answers you get! First memorise the few 'key' and 'secondary' questions below. Then, **always follow up your key question with a secondary question demanding a yes ('evet') or no ('hayir') answer.**

Following are the two most likely situations in which you may need to use some Turkish. The dots (…) show where you fill in the name of your destination. *See Index for Turkish spellings of place names and pronunciation.*

Asking the way
The key questions

English	Approximate Turkish pronunciation
Hello. Please —	**Merr**-haba. **Lewt**-fen —
Where is the road to …?	Yol nerede**deer**?
Where is the footpath to …?	Patika nerede**deer**?
Where is the bus stop?	Oto**bus** duraa eeneh-reh-**deh**?

Secondary questions leading to a yes/no answer

English	Approximate Turkish pronunciation
Is it here?	Bu-**rah**-dah me-**deer**?
Is it there? (fairly near)	Su-**rah**-dah me-**deer**?
Is it there? (more distant)	Or-**ah**-dah me-**deer**?
Is it straight ahead?	Doo-**ru** yolda me-**yeez**?
Is it behind?	Geh-ree-**deh** me-**deer**?
Is it to the right?	Bu sah-ah-**dah** me-**deer**?
Is it to the left?	Bu sol-**dah** me-**deer**?
Is it above?	Eu-steun-**deh** me-**deer**?
Is it below?	Al-tun-**dah** me-**deer**?
Thank you.	Teshehkewr ehdehreem.

Asking a taxi driver to take you somewhere and return for you, or asking a taxi driver to collect you somewhere

English	Approximate Turkish pronunciation
Please —	**Lewt**-fen —
would you take us to…?	Boo-**noo** bee-**zeem** ee-cheen al-**unuz**…?
Come and pick us up	Bee-**zee** tek-rahr ger-**eeyeh**
at … (time)	yurt-ur-oo**nooz** …

(Point to the time on your watch, or write it down.)

Organisation of the walks

Of the twenty-three main walks in this book, eleven are around Bodrum and twelve around Marmaris. You might begin by considering the large fold-out touring map between pages 14 and 15. Here you can see at a glance the overall terrain, the road network and the exact orientation of the walking maps in the text. Quickly flipping through the pages, you will find that there is at least one photograph for each walk.

Having selected one or two potential excursions from the map and the photographs, look over the planning information at the beginning of each walk. Here you'll find *our* walking times, grade, equipment and how to get there and return. If the grade and equipment specifications are beyond your scope, don't despair! *There's almost always a short or alternative version of the walk*, and in most cases, these are less demanding of ability and equipment. If it still looks too strenuous for you, turn to pages 9-12, where the picnic suggestions allow you to savour a walk's special landscape with minimum effort.

When you are on the walk, you'll find that the text begins with an introduction to the landscape and a comment on special points of interest before describing the route in detail. The text is illustrated with **large-scale maps** (all 1:50 000 and all orientated north/south).

Note that **we are very fit walkers** and that our times average between 3 and 6 kilometres an hour. Also note that the times given are *walking* times and include only brief pauses where you might stop to recover breath. They do *not* include photographic or picnic stops, or any stop of indeterminate length. So, if you are a beginner or simply out for a more leisurely stroll, *a walk may take you up to twice as long* as the stated time. Don't forget to take bus connections at the end of the walk into account, particularly with regard to the last bus or *dolmus*. The most important factor is *consistency* of walking times and we have made an effort to check our times at least twice. You'll soon see how your pace compares with ours and make adjustments for your stride ... and the heat!

These symbols are used on the walking maps:

═══ roads (red); tracks	----- footpath
◄─●/▲ water source, tap/*sarnic*	▬▬▬ route of walk (green)
P picnic spot (see pages 9-12)	🚗 car parking
✦/⳨ mosque/cemetery	⛽ petrol station
⣿/⣿ ancient site/ruins	👁 best views
▢ habitations	▪ specific building in text
1000 height in metres	🚌 bus or *dolmus* stop

A country code for walkers and motorists

The experienced rambler is used to following a 'country code', but the tourist out for a lark may unwittingly cause damage, harm animals, and even endanger his own life. Do heed this advice:

- **Do not light fires**. *Ates yakmak yasaktir* means that it is forbidden to light fires.
- **Do not frighten animals**. By making loud noises or trying to touch them or photograph them, you may cause them to run in fear and be hurt.
- **Walk quietly** through all farms, hamlets and villages, **leaving all gates just as you found them.**
  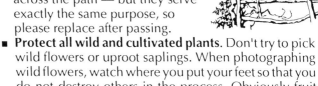
  Gates do have a purpose. Remember, too, that gates may be of a temporary nature — brushwood across the path — but they serve exactly the same purpose, so please replace after passing.
- **Protect all wild and cultivated plants**. Don't try to pick wild flowers or uproot saplings. When photographing wild flowers, watch where you put your feet so that you do not destroy others in the process. Obviously fruit and crops are someone's private property and should not be touched. *Never walk over cultivated land.*
- **Take all your litter away with you**.
- **Do not take risks**. Do not attempt walks beyond your capacity and *never* walk alone. *Always* tell a responsible person *exactly* where you are going and what time you plan to return. Remember, if you become lost or injure yourself, it may be a long time before you are found. On any but a very short walk near to villages, it's a good idea to take along a torch, a whistle and a compass, as well as extra food and clothing.
- Other points to remember:
  — **at any time a walk may become unsafe** due to storm damage or the havoc caused by bulldozers;
  — **strenuous walks** are unsuitable in high summer;
  — **do not overestimate your energy**: your speed will be determined by the slowest walker in your group;
  — **transport** at the end of the walk is important;
  — **proper shoes** or boots are a necessity;
  — **warm clothing** is needed in the moutains;
  — always take a **sunhat** with you, and cover arms and legs as well; don't be deceived by light cloud cover; you can still get sunburnt;
  — beware of **dehydration**; take ample fruit and water.

1 AKCAALAN TO AKYARLAR

Distance: 9km/5.6mi; 1h45min

Grade: easy-moderate. The walk is mainly over footpaths, often stony underfoot, and there is some climbing in the first part — up to 275m/900ft.

Equipment: sturdy shoes or boots, long-sleeved shirt, long trousers, sunglasses, suncream, cardigan, raingear, swimming costume, picnic and water

How to get there: 🚌 *dolmus* from Bodrum to the Akcaalan *yolu* (road), using the Bodrum/Turgutreis service, frequent departures (see timetable section). Journey time 20min
To return: 🚌 *dolmus*, first from Akyarlar to Turgutreis, then from there back to Bodrum

Shorter walks

1 Akcaalan to Karabag (5km/3mi; 1h; easy; good shoes and sun protection is all you need in the way of equipment). Follow the notes for the main walk as far as the village of Karabag. Return along the surfaced road by which you entered the village, but follow it all the way down, to join the main road just outside Turgutreis. Turn left here to continue down to the sea front.

2 Akcaalan to the windmills (8.5km/5.3mi; 1h45min; same grade and same equipment as the main walk). Follow the notes for the main walk, but go only as far as the windmills. Return by going back through the village of Karabag directly to Turgutreis, as in Short walk 1.

The *dolmus* journey out to Akcaalan takes you westwards from Bodrum through the village of Ortakent, or 'middle town', to give it its English name. Once beyond Ortakent notice how the scenery changes. The greenery-cloaked, rounded hills of limestone, so familiar around Bodrum, are replaced by the open volcanic landscape that covers the whole of the western half of the peninsula. As if to emphasise the starkness of the landscape, a tree might find a foothold. The hollows at a lower level collect and hold the soils washed down from the mountainsides, sometimes forming areas large enough for cultivation.

Viewpoints open up as you start to climb, with a fine panorama to enjoy back towards Akcaalan and the mosque near the start of the walk.

Imagine such a pocket of cultivation — an emerald green meadow, walled in brown stone; imagine it with a solitary white farmhouse built on the very edge, so that it takes up little or none of the valuable land for cultivation; picture the white farm with the luxury of a little shade from the single tall leafy green tree. See all this in your mind's eye against the brown barren hills rising steeply behind, and you have an image of the dramatic contrasts which are so typical of this intriguing landscape. This walk follows an old route between two lovely villages, passing on the way some delightful old windmills which grace the skyline almost from the start. At the end of the walk there is the quaint fishing village of Akyarlar to explore.

Ask to leave the *dolmus* at the road leading up to Akcaalan, the 'Akcaalan *yolu'*. It is the second of two roads on the left, located by the sign for Turgutreis, and is reached just as you crest the brow of the hill to start the long straight stretch of road leading to the sea. **Start out** by heading up the road into the village of Akcaalan and continue without deviation until you pass the mosque on the right in **5min**; then turn right into Okul Sokak (School St). A little way down the street, there is a tower house (see drawing on page 63) on the right, reached in **7min**. Take the track running ahead to the right, between the tower house and the school, passing a *sarnic* (water container; see Walk 3, page 61) on the left almost immediately. The village is soon left behind and, looking ahead, you can see three windmills on the skyline. Ignore the path off left, reached in **10min**, and stay with the track as it swings right and shortly becomes walled-in on both sides. There is a lovely pastoral feel to the walk, as you head through well-tended farmlands. Viewpoints open up as you climb until, in **17min**, you have the fine view shown on page 49.

Shortly (**21min**) the track swings to the right to join a narrow road on a bend, where you turn left. A minute up this road gives you your first view of the village of Karabag above; it's perched on a platform nestling into the hillside. Higher to the right are the windmills. Continue up into the village to reach first a water fountain with a tap and then a mosque on the left (**28min**). Keep straight ahead here to join a track, where the concrete road leads away to the left. When the track forks, in less than a minute, stay left and then swing sharp right, ignoring the smaller track which continues ahead on this corner. The village is now down on the right as you cross above it, passing another fountain on the left in **31min**. Keep straight on as the track reduces on the outskirts of the village and leads into a walled-in path. You briefly head back in the direction of the sea. Watch out for the sharp left turn uphill in **34min**, when you reach a ruined house: leave the walls behind, to head up the open hillside towards the windmills. Immediately in front, a wall appears to bar your way. But, as you approach the wall two minutes later, keep to the left, to enter a wide walled-in trail. Then turn right (**38min**), to continue on a very stony trail. Looking back now there are good views over Karabag and, as you climb a little higher, you can see a skyline of seven windmills in the direction of Gumusluk.

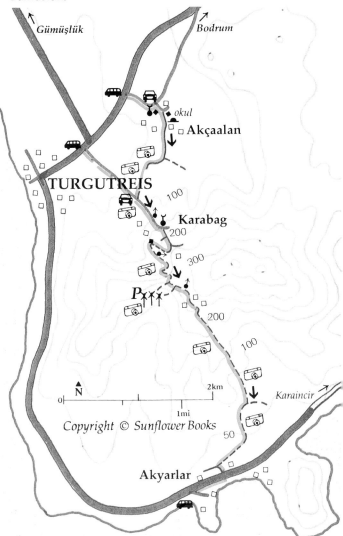

Take care in **43min** to follow the stony trail as it leads you away from the wall on the right and up to the left of the windmills — again between confining walls. Follow the walled-in trail through a couple of swings to the right, to reach a junction of paths just below the windmills (**48min**); here fork left. The opportunity to inspect the windmills and enjoy some spectacular views comes up a minute later, when you take a path up right to reach them (**51min**). Looking at the craggy hilltop surrounded by pink-hued rocky terrain over to the east, the eye can just make out the remains of buildings which blend so well in this hostile environment. These may well be part of ancient Termera, which is known to be in this region.

Head back from the windmills and turn right when you reach the point of diversion (**53min**). Follow the path to continue along the line of the wall on the left, passing a small fountain set in the wall four minutes later. Eye-catching splashes of yellow and green lichen decorate the rosy-hued rocks as you pass over this high part of the walk. As you approach a partly-ruined hamlet after **1h**, follow the path as it passes close to a ruin on the right; ahead you enjoy views of the southern coast. Within three minutes the path becomes walled-in for a time where, on the right, *Opuntia* has been planted to act as a hedge. As you start your descent, in **1h6min**, the path loses its clear identity over an area of bedrock; stay more or less down the middle, heading in the direction of the hilly promontory clustered with white apartments that you can see ahead. The enclosing walls are set wide apart now but, when you clear the bedrock, you will find that you are funnelled back into a narrow walled-in trail.

You meet a junction of trails in **1h24min**. Turn right here, to descend the rocky walled-in trail; it ends in a wide grassy area. Follow a path along the line of the right-hand wall, still heading for the base of the headland. From here you look down on Akyarlar and towards Kos. It looks for a moment as if there may be no way out, as you approach a walled-in corner (**1h33min**), but there is a gap on the right for you to pass through. Keep uphill momentarily, then cut down diagonally towards a track which you meet on a corner (**1h40min**). Go down left here, to reach the main road a minute later. You can catch a *dolmus* here, if one is passing, but it is better to turn right on the road to reach Akyarlar's shore in a further three minutes. Here you can swim or enjoy refreshments (in the season), while waiting for the *dolmus*.

2 GUMUSLUK • KARAKAYA • GUMUSLUK

Distance: 8.5km/5.3mi; 1h35min   See also cover photograph

Grade: easy, but be warned that the paths are very stony underfoot and there is a little uphill work to do.

Equipment: sturdy shoes or boots, long-sleeved shirt, long trousers, sunglasses, suncream, cardigan, raingear, swimming costume, picnic and water

How to get there: 🚌 *dolmus* from Bodrum to Gumusluk main village (see below), frequent departures (see timetable section). Journey time 25-30min

To return: 🚌 *dolmus* back to Bodrum, either from the coast or from Gumusluk main village

Shorter walk: To the windmill and return (5.7km/3.5mi; 1h 10min; same grade and equipment). Follow the notes for the main walk, but go only as far as the windmill. Return by the same route, then continue down to the coast, as in the main walk.

R ickety wooden landing jetties in the unhurried sweep of the bay … a waterside café or two … a scattering of white buildings … and a peaceful unchanging life-style — this is Gumusluk. This totally unspoilt fishing village, shown on the cover of the book, has been denied growth because of the archaeological importance of nearby Myndos. And the local people prefer it that way. Traffic too is kept outside the village, but there is a car park.

This short walk has been designed to leave you time to enjoy the peaceful ambience of Gumusluk, perhaps to enjoy refreshments at a waterside café and wander around to look at the remains of Myndos (such as they are: there is actually little to see of it, since most of the ruins are now under the sea). You might also visit 'rabbit island', where almost-tame rabbits run around freely. The rabbits are bred by one of the locals and, while the island is joined to the mainland by a causeway for much of the year, the causeway is removed in the tourist season to discourage too many visitors. It is no problem if you want to go, but it does mean that you have to paddle across in summer — and the water may be up to your knees in places.

The lovely windmill en route to Karakaya (Picnic 2b)

The walk itself takes you to one of the loveliest windmills on the peninsula (see page 53) and, like Walk 1, explores the dramatic landscapes in this fascinating volcanic region. Gumusluk takes its name from the Turkish word for silver, and there is evidence of old silver mines nearby. Like a number of coastal villages on this peninsula, it is actually divided into two, with part of the village by the sea but the main part well inland. The two parts are separated, in this case, by a distance of just over 1km. You will leave the *dolmus* at inland Gumusluk to start the walk. The *dolmus* driver (who expects to take tourists only to the coast) may try to dissuade you: say '*tamam*' ('okay'), to reassure him....

Alight by the mosque in the main village and **start the walk** by following the direction of the departing *dolmus* for a short time — to where the buildings finish on the right. Turn sharp right here, into an old trail leading up behind the buildings. You pass a *sarnic* (water container; see Walk 3, page 61) on the left and, in **3min**, you join a track coming from the right (on a bend). Here keep straight ahead. Leave the track by a fountain, in **6min**, to turn right into a trail which takes you over a very rocky area, heading for a farm gate. The trail leads you up and around to the left of the farm, and you continue climbing steadily. The shade of tall holly oaks is soon lost as you reach an area of open bedrock in **10min**. Continue towards the solitary white pumping station ahead, by keeping to an indistinct path which winds up over the bedrock: stay to the right,

Copyright © *Sunflower Books*

and you will pick up a narrow path. The pumping station, reached in **14min**, is a good place to catch your breath and admire the views: a line of seven windmills on the hilltop to the east catch the eye, as do the off-shore islands — of which Kos is the larger one. The three windmills silhouetted on the skyline to the south are visited in Walk 1.

Thorny burnett, *Sarcopoterium spinosum*, giving a realistic impression of wire netting bushes, dot the way now along this stony enclosed section of path, which opens up again before you reach a fork (**22min**). Take the left-hand path which leads up through the cutting, to give you a compelling view of Karakaya less than a minute later. The village clings to the hostile slopes of a rocky mountain, overlooking the green and fertile valley floor. From here the path heads right towards Karakaya, but first divert left to visit the windmill. Climb over the wall, without disturbing the reinforcing brushwood, and take the path leading around to the right side of and just below this small ridge. Giant fennel, *Ferula communis*, borders the path. You reach the summit and the windmill in **26min**. Flower-filled meadows provide a perfect setting for this lovely old mill that once used to grind corn. Return by the same route, taking care not to miss the path down off the summit, soon after leaving the windmill.

Back on the main path (**31min**), follow it towards Karakaya, keeping at first to the edge of the plain and then swinging around to the left, to cross a stream. Reach a junction of paths beneath the village in **40min**. If you explore Karakaya, return to this junction and follow the continuation of the path below the village. It leads into a steeply-descending trail, quickly taking you out of sight of Karakaya and into an open rocky area. Descend here, generally following the line of the wall on the left, until you meet up with the wall when it swings right at the bottom. You swing right here also, to pick up the trail again. There are some captivating views of rocky formations over to the right, as you cross the stream in **50min**, and a new softness comes into the landscape — especially in spring, when you glimpse the fields shown overleaf, white with Greek chamomile, *Anthemis chia*. A fountain in a large grassy area is reached in **57min**. Continue ahead to cross a stream bed. Ignore the track which leads off to the right in **1h**. A moment later, as you pass a water trough on the left, keep left by the wall, to find yourself shortly back on a walled-in path, with a stream to the left. Dip down to cross the stream and continue ahead, back into the walled-in path, to reach a cross-path in **1h9min**. Here turn left into another narrow walled-in path and pass a tap on the left. The minaret at Gumusluk is now in view ahead and very soon, in **1h13min**, you are back at the fountain you passed 6min into the walk. Keep straight ahead here, into the track/trail which leads you back to the main road at the point where you started out (**1h20min**). Turn right here to head for the shore, some 15 minutes away.

Greek chamomile softens the harshness of the volcanic landscape.

3 YALIKAVAK • SANDIMA • GERIS • YALIKAVAK

Distance: 11.9km/7.4mi; 2h20min   **See also photos pages 63, 64, 67**

Grade: moderate. Many of the paths and trails used in this walk are stony underfoot, and there is some climbing — from sea level up to an elevation of 300m/1000ft.

Equipment: sturdy shoes or boots, long-sleeved shirt, long trousers, sunglasses, suncream, cardigan, raingear, swimming costume, picnic and water

How to get there: 🚌 *dolmus* from Bodrum to Yalikavak, departures fairly frequent (see timetable section). Journey time 25min
To return: 🚌 *dolmus* from Yalikavak to Bodrum

Short walk: Yalikavak—Sandima—Yalikavak (5.5km/3.4mi; 1h10min; easy-moderate; use same equipment). Follow the main walk as far as Sandima and return the same way.

An adequate supply of water, for crops, for animals and for man, has been one of the major problems of survival in the arid volcanic western region of the Bodrum peninsula. There is no shortage of rain in winter but, with no great depth of soil to hold or store the water, there is need for some other system, hence the *sarnic*. The *sarnic*, or *gumbet*, is a lovely domed structure for storing water. It is often plastered and painted white. You will see many of these around the peninsula, but there is a particularly fine one along this walk; it is shown on page 61.

Apart from some glorious coastal views which stay with you for a good length of time as you climb above Yalikavak, there are also two villages en route which are captivating for quite different reasons. Sandima is situated in a bowl, at the base of a ring of barren hills, and is totally inaccessible to wheeled traffic. It is now largely deserted and may well have been another of the Greek villages vacated during the 1922 exchange of populations. The occasional splash of green from a cultivated meadow, or the glimpse of an old woman bowed under the weight of sticks stealing silently down a far pathway, are reminders that this existence is a way of life for some. Geris, in contrast, shines white and exudes vitality from its hilltop position. The local people there are very friendly, and we had some difficulty passing through without taking tea or stopping to take requested photographs....

Yalikavak, shown on page 63, is only a small village, but it is important for sponge-fishing and provides most of the sponges for Turkey. It has a small beach, too, from where you can swim. Leave the *dolmus* at the terminus in Yalikavak (which is the main square). **Start the walk** from here by heading down the road between the mosque and the toilets. In only a few yards, as you pass the cemetery on the left, the road reduces to track and instantly you are in a country lane heading through the orange groves towards Sandima. Keep straight on, ignoring the two tracks joining from the right (but note that the second of these, reached in **8min**, is the return route). Once through a small hamlet reached in **12min**, the track continues as an old trail running alongside a stream on the left. Masses of *Opuntia* bring a different character to the countryside, in spite of the presence of the more familiar olive tree. The way varies between path and trail for a time but, in **15min**, the path dips to cross a small sidestream before continuing in a steady ascent. The views begin to open up as you climb and, by the time you reach the *sarnic* in **20min**, it is worth a stop to enjoy both the panorama and the setting of this picturesque water container, shown on page 61. Flowers decorate the way here — wherever the soil depths allow them a

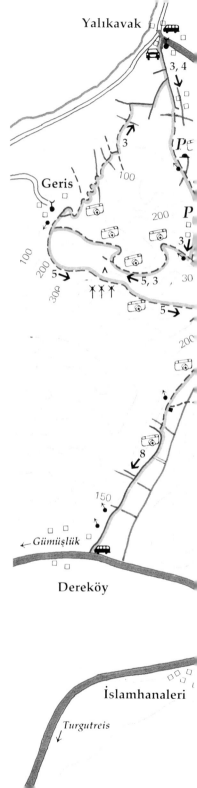

Gölköy →

Gökcebel

150 ← 5

74
6
7

Sandıma

Dağbelen

200

300   4, 5

250

okul

Yaka

150

200

4, 5

8

8

Bodrum →

Ortakent

100

Gürece

Yahşi

N

2km

0

1mi

Copyright © Sunflower Books

foothold, from the wild orchids like *Orchis sancta*, the holy orchid, to the more shrubby fringed rue, *Ruta chalapensis*, which grows around the fountain reached four minutes later. The stream which you have been following on the left changes course — which means that you now cross it (**27min**), to continue in a steady ascent.

Alpine gardeners may well eat their hearts out at the sight of some delightfully-shaped stone troughs scattered around the well on the approach to Sandima, reached in **30min**. Silence hangs heavily around the nearly deserted village, creating an atmosphere of the unreal, as though you have just walked onto a huge stage set. Photographic opportunities abound. (There is a photograph of Sandima, but taken from the route of Walk 4, on page 64.) As you first enter the village there is a large grassy area (Walk 5 comes in here), by a walled-in graveyard and some tall eucalyptus trees over to the right. This is a delightful spot with fine views, where you might be tempted to picnic.

To continue from here, head right, aiming for the eucalyptus trees. But turn sharp left, into a walled-in trail, just before reaching them. Head uphill, almost due south, through the right-hand side of the village. You reach an ornamental water fountain in **33min**. The small bore metal pipe which supplies the fountain with water acts as a useful guide for a time: continue in a fairly steep ascent following the line of the pipe, in two minutes passing a running water source and a trough on the left. The path is somewhat indistinct over the hard rock, but keep the pipe and a wall on your left until, in **38min**, you cross the pipe before it terminates. This a good place to catch your breath for a moment and take in the captivating views back over Sandima. The climb becomes more gradual as you press on, keeping a wall on the right, and you find that you are being channelled into a walled-in trail (see photograph page 67). There are cultivated terraces on each side here and, after passing a farmstead on the left, you reach a junction of trails (**45min**), where you turn right. Follow the walled-in path, drinking in the superb coastal views as you go. But be sure not to miss the sharp left turn, in **54min**, when the path doubles back on itself at a higher level. There is a fine view of Sandima from this point, and, above the village, you can see the rich meadow ('*yayla*') which once sustained it. See also how the flat-topped houses are built on the naked rock to preserve the productive land. This is the highest point of the walk (**56min**).

Ahead now is a beautiful fertile valley, where walled

Rain falling on the outer dome of this sarnic below Sandima is channelled to the excavated interior, where it is protected from the evaporating rays of the sun. A door and steps inside the dome give access to the water. (Picnic 3a)

terraces weave their own patterns into the landscape. Geris comes into view only moments later, glistening white in the sun from its hilltop position. From here the route of our walled-in path to Geris is easily seen. Watch out for a sharp turn at the fork met in **1h10min**, but stay within the walled-in path. The descent steepens through a zig-zag for a time, leading you down to cross the valley floor and a dry stream bed (**1h18min**). You then swing right and start uphill towards Geris. At the junction of trails, in **1h24min**, turn right to head into Geris (but turn left for Walk 5), arriving in the village square in **1h30min**.

Cross the square diagonally to the right-hand corner and go down between the houses, to find the start of the trail which will lead you back to Yalikavak. Ignore the trail joining from the right almost immediately and continue in a steep descent, keeping watch for a path to the right indicated by a red arrow (**1h36min**). This stony path, enclosed by walls, drops you down to a stream in a small wooded valley splashed pink with oleander. Descend to cross the stream (**1h43min**), and then climb through a shaded plant-tunnel, where old, gnarled olive trees and lush green fennel lead the way back into a walled-in path. Another stream is crossed just moments before reaching a fork (**1h49min**), where you go right — only to fork left almost immediately. The countryside here announces its fertility with drifts of springtime colours — red from the *Anemone coronaria* and white from the daisy *Anthemis chia.* You're accompanied by the enchanting song of the nightingale. Contrast this to the earlier part of the walk.

It is a relief to walk on a smooth path for a time, but soon it is again stony underfoot. Continue along the water seepage, reached in **2h**, to cross a stream less than a minute later. Come to a cross-track in **2h5min**: turn right and follow this rough track, gently ascending through citrus groves and then dropping down to meet another track in **2h11min**. Here turn left. One more left turn, at the next junction (**2h14min**), brings you back to the main square in Yalikavak and to the return *dolmus.*

4 YALIKAVAK • SANDIMA • YAKA • ORTAKENT

See map pages 58-59; see also photograph page 61

Distance: 12km/7.5mi; 2h17min

Grade: moderate. Many of the paths and trails used in this walk are stony, and there is some uphill work, from sea level to 300m/1000ft.

Equipment: sturdy shoes or boots, long-sleeved shirt, long trousers, sunglasses, suncream, cardigan, raingear, picnic and water

How to get there: 🚐 *dolmus* from Bodrum to Yalikavak, departures fairly frequent (see timetable section). Journey time 25min
To return: 🚐 any *dolmus* from Ortakent back to Bodrum

Shorter walk: Yalikavak—Yaka (9.8km/6.1mi; 1h50min; same grade, same equipment). Follow the notes for the main walk until you reach the track at Yaka in 1h27min. Turn left here and follow the track until it emerges on the Yalikavak road, where you can wait for a *dolmus* to take you back to Bodrum.

A part from some dramatic scenery with weird rock formations, villages add considerable interest to this walk. The seemingly quiet village of Yalikavak, where the walk starts, is actually famous for its sponges, and it is not unusual to see large catches spread out in the sun to dry. Not only does the village supply Bodrum with its sponges, it is also one of the largest suppliers in Turkey. Next along the route is the now-deserted, but very photogenic village of Sandima (described in Walk 3). Heading south from Sandima, you cross over a hill to Yaka. If there is such a thing as a typical Turkish village untouched by tourism on this western part of the Bodrum peninsula, then it must be Yaka. Connected to the road system only by a dirt track, Yaka sits near the top of a hillside, looking down over the pastures which sustain it. If you are looking for shops or any other facilities, then steel yourself until you reach Ortakent. Ortakent is another of those villages which exist in two parts, one inland and one by the sea. Our walk ends at inland Ortakent. If you have time in hand, then it is worth having a look around to see some fine examples of old Turkish architecture, including the Mustafa Pasa tower house which dates from 1601. To reach the Ortakent

Yalikavak

62

beach from here requires a further journey by *dolmus*.

To **begin the walk**, leave the *dolmus* at the terminus (main square) in Yalikavak. Use the notes for Walk 3 (page 57) to reach the beginnings of Sandima (**30min**). Here Walk 4 continues ahead: ignore the path down on the left, just past the enclosed graveyard, and enter the confines of a walled-in path. Looking down to the

A 17th-century tower house characteristic of Ortakent

left as you climb, the steep valley (photograph page 64), is brightened by pockets of pink oleander, prickly pear cactus (*Opuntia ficus-indica*), and the century plant (*Agave americana*). This last has enormous rosettes, easily a metre in diameter, formed of thick grey-green, sword-like leaves. The flower spike, which takes several years to form, resembles a telegraph pole in height and thickness.

The path heads straight up the valley, passing to the right of a ruined building (**35min**), to continue shortly as a walled-in path again. Although the path does maintain a steady route over the area of bedrock reached in **39min**, the enclosing walls widen to follow an erratic course

around the boundaries of the rocky area and are less useful as 'waymarkers' — particularly in **44min**, when you need to keep up and to the the right of a rocky outcrop. Still ascending steadily, the narrow path crosses an area of typical small shrubby phrygana. Turn left in **52min**, when you meet a stream, and follow it for a short distance. Then leave the stream bed on the right-hand side, again following a walled-in path. You ascend more steeply, keeping the densely vegetated, narrow valley down on your left. At the crest of the hill (**1h**) you meet a junction where Walk 5 joins from the right: turn left and, almost immediately, right, to continue up onto a saddle, from where there are new vistas down to the southern coastline.

Now descending, the path divides briefly into many ways to cross a slippery area of loose stone and shale (**1h3min**). Soon afterwards the walls enclose the path, to guide you securely in a slow and steady descent along the hillside of a lovely fertile valley. A few houses from the village of Dagbelen can be seen peeping over the hillside on the far left, and below you can see the main road leading to Yalikavak. But as yet Yaka is hidden from view. It remains so until you are almost upon it. On meeting the main track, in **1h29min**, turn right to head into Yaka (but turn left for the Shorter walk). Keep left at the branching of tracks two minutes later, just after passing the school on

Leaving Sandima, a largely deserted and lonely village: for a time you walk uphill over bare rock. Looking down to the left, you can see the steep valley which divides the village in two. Curiously-sculptured rock forms catch the eye further over to the left.

the left. Less than a minute from this junction (**1h32min**), turn sharp left onto a path and keep heading downhill; a hedged wall on the right and a barbed wire fence on the left guide you for a time. When the path divides, in **1h37**, the choice is yours; the forks rejoin very shortly. Ignore the path which joins from the right two minutes later and continue ahead, to across a dry stream bed and reach a huge plane tree (**1h40min**). Its trunk has divided into three parts, and the path passes through the middle of the tree....

Continue ahead, with the dry stream bed — and soon a flowing stream — on your right, to find walls enclosing the path again. Cross the stream in **1h43min** and continue via a walled-in path. At **1h48min** the path runs into the stream for a time, and it is necessary to weave along the stream using the short stretches of path on the left whenever possible. You emerge near greenhouses (photograph page 79) two minutes later, climbing away from the stream to a large open area. Continue ahead, towards the left-hand corner, passing a huge plane tree and crossing over a track to enter a walled-in path. There is more stony bedrock to cross before you pass a walled-in path leading off to the right (**1h54min**; the route of walk 8). You emerge from within the walls to walk by a dry stream bed on the right. Filtered sunlight throws dappled shadows on a lovely wooded section of the path (**1h57min**), before you cross the dry stream bed on the right to reach a confluence of stream beds in **2h**. Turn right here to keep the large stream bed on the left for a few moments — until the path leads you down to criss-cross the very stony bed.

You will emerge on the far bank with the stream bed on your right. Just before you reach a well (**2h4min**), swing left into a sunken walled-in path which provides plenty of shade. Some three minutes later, the walled-in path is left behind, and you emerge into an open area by a water-pumping station on the left. Turn right here, to enter another walled-in path running between cultivated fields. Soon, in **2h10min**, you must turn right, by a house on the right, heading again into a walled-in path. It leads you to a dry stream bed in a minute. Head left here, first along the dry stream bed, and then onto the path on the right of the stream. Reach another confluence of two streams, both usually dry, where three piers from an ancient bridge still stand. Cross this junction, heading for the walled-in path to the left. It takes you into Ortakent (**2h17min**). Cross the main road at the point where you emerge, to wait for the *dolmus* back to Bodrum.

5 *YEL DEGIRMENLERI* • SANDIMA • (GERIS) • YAKA • ORTAKENT

See map on pages 58-59; see also photographs pages 61, 63, 64

Distance: 18.9km/11.8mi; 3h46min

Grade: moderate-strenuous. There are two sections of uphill work to contend with, the harder one taking you up to 350m/1150ft, and the footpaths are often very stony underfoot.

Equipment: sturdy shoes or boots, long-sleeved shirt, long trousers, sunglasses, suncream, cardigan, raingear, picnic and water

How to get there: 🚐 *dolmus* from Bodrum using the Bodrum/Yalikavak service, departures fairly frequent (see timetable section). Journey time about 20min. Leave the *dolmus* at the windmills (see below).

To return: 🚐 any *dolmus* from Ortakent back to Bodrum

Short walks: There are a number of variations to this walk, since it links up with both Walks 3 and 4. Amongst the possibilities are

1 *Yel degirmenleri* — Sandima — Yalikavak (6.5km/4mi; 1h10min; easy; same equipment). Follow the notes for the main walk, to reach Sandima in 40min; then join Walk 3 just below the cemetery (the 30min-point in Walk 3) and use those notes in reverse, to walk from Sandima down to Yalikavak. Return to Bodrum by *dolmus* from Yalikavak.

2 *Yel degirmenleri* — Sandima — Yaka (11km/6.9mi; 2h5min; moderate; same equipment). Use the notes for the main walk to reach Sandima (40min). Join the route of Walk 3, and follow it to climb away from Sandima towards Geris. But go only as far as the junction of trails reached at the 45min-point in Walk 3. Turn left here and continue climbing, to reach a junction in the path 10min later. Here you rejoin the route of Walk 5, but at the 2h18min-point. Turn left, using the notes on page 68. Go as far as Yaka but, when you join the track into Yaka, turn left for the main road, where you can catch the *dolmus* back to Bodrum.

3 *Yel degirmenleri* — Sandima — Geris — Yaka (16.7km/10.4mi; 3h18min; grade and equipment as main walk). Follow the main walk as far as Yaka but, when you join the track leading into Yaka, turn left to the main road, where you can await the *dolmus* back to Bodrum.

*Y*el degirmenleri, 'windmills', have a charm of their own, evoking romantic images of a rustic age when sails turned lazily, and life moved at a much slower pace. Life still does move at a slower pace in these parts, especially in the hill villages and the high *yaylas* (meadows).

Leave the *dolmus* at the windmills which lie just beyond the track to Dagbelen, but before the descent into Yalikavak. **Start the walk** as you leave the *dolmus* by heading down the road in the same direction, to feast your eyes immediately on the absorbing coastal views over Yalikavak. When you reach a bend, in **9min**, look on the left for the path which leads down across a stream and follow it into a walled-in path. Shortly, where the path divides to negotiate an area of exposed bedrock, stay to the left (by the wall) and continue along the footpath into a winding descent. Be sure to stay up left, near the wall, as you descend; don't be tempted by the minor paths down to the right.

Walks 3 and 5: Climbing above Sandima en route to Geris, we enter a walled-in trail with coastal views down over Yalikavak.

A change of direction comes up in **17min**, as the path describes a sharp right turn when you meet the stream. Continue with the stream on your left for a time, but cross it in **20min** and follow it only briefly — before swinging left to enter another walled-in section of the path. The confining walls guide you into a diagonal ascent away from the stream, which is now down to your right.

Views open out as you climb. Looking back you can see a further two windmills along the ridge from where this walk started and, in the immediate surrounds, the line of the walled-in path stretching ahead is clearly etched on the landscape. There is an area of exposed bedrock to negotiate just before reaching a rocky outcrop in **28min**. (If you divert briefly to the right here, there is an inviting area of flat rock, where you might be tempted to picnic if the sun is not too strong. It offers delightful views over both Yalikavak and Sandima.)

Continue along the path as it swings left through a narrow cutting only a minute later, to emerge overlooking Sandima nestling in the huge valley below. On the left in this striking picture is a white *sarnic* (water container; see Walk 3, page 61), over to the right some fantastic rock formations and, in the foreground, enclosed green meadows highlight the starkness of the surrounds. From the *sarnic* (**31min**) the path leads down over the bedrock towards the village, described in Walk 3 and shown in the photograph on page 64. As you enter the village, swing down right towards the valley bottom, finally taking a sharp left turn to cross the stream in **38min**. A second, smaller stream is crossed a minute later, as you climb into the main part of the village, where you meet a junction of paths by the graveyard (**40min**). A left turn here leads into Walk 4, but our way lies to the right, and we round the graveyard, to reach a large grassy area almost immediately. Swing left now towards the eucalyptus trees (but keep straight down for Short walk 5-1 to Yalikavak) and, almost immediately, turn left to enter a walled-in trail.

Now use the notes for Walk 3 on page 60 (the 30min-point), until the junction of trails is reached just outside Geris (**1h34min**; the 1h24min-point in Walk 3). Turn left here, away from Geris. The trail quickly degenerates into a less obvious stony path, as it heads diagonally uphill to meet a wall on the left at the top of the rise three minutes later. Continue with the wall on your left, and stay left when the path divides briefly (**1h42min**), to swing around the head of the valley. Ignore the paths going down left now; keep up right over the exposed bedrock. You reach a point where there is a wall on your right (**1h48min**); continue with it on your right. When you arrive at a huge rock with a hole in its base (**1h51min**), it is worthwhile to take a breather and enjoy the views over towards the peninsula beyond Yalikavak.

From here follow the path uphill to reach the top of the ridge (**1h57min**), and continue along the ridge, with fine views. After passing through a small clump of pines, the path becomes walled-in, but soon continues with a wall only on the right. The skyline to the left is dominated by a massive angular rock, which is a useful landmark, as the path heads in that direction. Continue following the path as it descends over stony ground, keeping a knoll on the right, still making towards the large angular rock, until you join a path by a wall on your right (**2h11min**).

Continue with the wall on your right and enjoy views of a fertile valley with red-roofed houses, where you can see the track from Yaka en route to Derekoy (Walk 8). A further six minutes sees you passing beneath the huge rock, towards Sandima's valley. Reach a junction of paths (**2h18min**), where you turn right (Short walk 5-2 joins in at this point). The path from here leads through low-domed phrygana, around the hillside and back into the confines of a walled-in path (**2h24min**), to reach a junction of paths. Here Walk 4 joins from the left. Now using the notes for Walk 4 (from the 1h-point), keep straight ahead and up to the right over the saddle. Carry on down to Yaka (**2h56min**) and Ortakent (**3h46min**).

6 DAGBELEN TO THE BITEZ *YOLU*

See map page 74

Distance: 12.2km/7.6mi; 2h25min

Grade: moderate. The tracks and paths used are varied, sometimes good underfoot, but often stony, and there is some climbing to an altitude of about 325m/1050ft, starting from around 150m/500ft.

Equipment: sturdy shoes or boots, long-sleeved shirt, long trousers, sunglasses, suncream, cardigan, raingear, picnic and water

How to get there: 🚐 *dolmus* to Dagbelen using the Bodrum/Yalikavak service, departures fairly frequent (see timetable section). Journey time about 18min

To return: 🚐 any passing *dolmus* back to Bodrum

This old route across the Bodrum peninsula is still the only means of communication with the partly-inhabited village shown on the next page — Kibrel, where old rose-coloured houses blend beautifully into the surrounding bare rock. Kibrel still supports a small community of goatherds. The obscure Lelegian town of Side is also thought to be in this region, and the ruins of the tower that we pass on route might be connected with it. An interesting characteristic of Lelegian architecture is the use of roughly-squared blocks for building so, should you stop at the old tower for a picnic, or just to rest, then you can cast a critical eye and make your own judgement.

Many of the people in this area aim at nothing more than self-sufficiency in their farming and very often have just one or two cows, perhaps a bull or a few goats. In the morning 'rush hour' there is a constant stream of villagers taking their farm stock out to graze, and you may see this in the early part of the walk. Even in the larger settlements, like Yalikavak, it is still not unusual to see farm stock being herded through the village centre. Should you see any cows that look as though they may have strayed, then do take note of it — on more than one occasion while out walking, we have been approached by a distraught villager asking if we had seen his lost cow.

Give Dagbelen as your destination on the *dolmus,* and you will be dropped off at the end of the track leading into

Near Dagbelen: Along any of the walks there is a reasonable chance of seeing a camel or a string of camels.

the village. **Start the walk** by heading up the wide track (on the same side as you leave the bus). The first houses of Dagbelen come into sight fairly soon, but it is not until you have passed a fountain on the left, in **14min**, and another on the left a minute later, that you get an overview of the place. It is typical of these parts in that it is built perched on a hillside overlooking fertile land used for cultivation. As you enter the village, in **16min**, you can see that it is very much inhabited, with a mixture of old and new houses.

Keep straight through Dagbelen until you reach a fork in the track (**20min**), where you go left. Almost immediately pass a fountain on the left. The track winds up to the higher part of the village, passing another fountain on the left (**22min**), before reducing to more of a trail. There are lovely pastoral views around as you climb up and away from Dagbelen, particularly over the hillside where the early morning sun filtering through the trees on the terraces produces an interesting play of light and shade. Continue as the now cobbled and walled-in trail winds its way uphill. Ignore the path down right in **28min**, and pass another fountain on the left in **32min**. Two minutes later you reach a crest. There are some views of the northern shore to absorb you here, before you start to descend into

Earlier glimpses of the partly-ruined village of Kibrel do nothing to prepare you for this unreal scene — only when it comes into full view, at 1h12min into the walk, can you appreciate the beauty of these pink houses scattered on a barren hillside in the middle of a wilderness.

pine woods where, in **40min**, you keep on the main trail, ignoring the crossing paths. When the trail swings right to a farm and ends, join the path which runs straight ahead. A wall and the farm are on the right. You reach a clearing with the ruins of an old tower some two minutes later (**46min**) — a lovely spot to picnic or just relax, with sea views through the pines on both sides of the peninsula.

Continue ahead alongside the clearing, to reach a junction of trails in **48min**, where you keep right (Walk 7 joins from the left here), starting into a further ascent. The trail takes a winding course towards the middle of the peninsula, heading to the right, above the farmstead, before swinging round left. Olive groves indicate the proximity of habitation, as you walk along a boundary wall on the right (**58min**). Ignore the path which joins from the left a minute later. A white *sarnic* (water container; see Walk 3, page 61) comes into view on the right very shortly, and the trail swings towards it, passing around an old graveyard on the left. There is plenty of shade from the huge specimen holly oak tree by the *sarnic*, should you want to rest or picnic here (**1h2min**). Continue along the walled-in trail, starting now to descend slightly over stony ground. At **1h9min** you come to a point where a path

branches off left to another *sarnic*, but where you keep straight on. Similarly, keep straight on a minute later at another branch-off to the left.

Earlier glimpses of the partly-ruined village of Kibrel do nothing to prepare you for the unreal scene of pink houses scattered on a barren hillside in the middle of a wilderness, when it comes into full view (**1h12min**; photograph page 71). At this point there is a stone building and a wall on the right; turn right immediately past this building, at the corner of the wall. Head downhill diagonally to the right, to join another path leading from the village just two minutes later: here turn right and pass a water hole on the left almost immediately. Follow the path which soon goes alongside a wall on the right, bordering a cultivated field and a house (**1h17min**). You come to a vantage point three minutes later where, if you look back, you can see the village blending well into its rocky surroundings and notice that the path has described almost a semi-circle around the cultivated area.

There is still a wall and a hedge on the right as you start to descend into the valley towards the southern coast. Follow the path as it swings around left, passing a dried-up water hole on the right (**1h23min**), to continue through the pine and phrygana in a steady descent. In spite of the stony and inhospitable ground, many of the meadows are still being worked, and olive trees are still around. A series of bends quickly brings you down to the valley bottom in **1h42min**; here you continue along a dry stony river bed — almost like walking on a shingle beach. The sides of the valley slowly close around you until, in **1h54min**, you find yourself walking through a very narrow and beautiful gorge which has straight-sided walls.

Emerging from the gorge eight minutes later, you come to the remains of a well or *sarnic* on the right. From here the path leads straight towards quarry workings, so some diversionary tactics are required. Continue ahead but, as the gully develops on your right, take an early opportunity to cross it, by taking the path down towards the small building on the right (**2h7min**). It is a bit of a scramble up the far bank by the fence but, once up, continue following the line of the gully (which is now on your left), until the path runs into a track leading past the quarry office (**2h19min**). Continue through part of the quarry, to meet the main road in **2h25min**. Cross over the road and wait for the *dolmus* back to Bodrum at the junction with the Bitez road (Bitez *yolu*).

Distance: 7.7km/4.8mi; 1h35min   **See photograph page 69**

Grade: moderate. There is a fair amount of uphill work, from sea level to 325m/1070ft, and often over stony paths.

Equipment: sturdy shoes or boots, long-sleeved shirt, long trousers, sunglasses, suncream, cardigan, raingear, picnic and water

How to get there: 🚐 *dolmus* from Bodrum to Gundogan, fairly frequent departures (see timetable section). Journey time about 20min
To return: 🚐 *dolmus* back to Bodrum, using the Yalikavak/Bodrum service

Alternative walk: Gundogan to the Bitez *yolu*: (11.7km/7.3mi; 2h25min; moderate-strenuous; same equipment). Follow the notes for the main walk until you join the Dagbelen/Bitez trail in 45min. Instead of turning right at this point, carry on straight ahead and use the notes for Walk 6 (from the 46min-point; page 71) to take you to the junction of the Bitez road (Bitez *yolu*) and the main road just west of Bodrum.

G undogan is another of those villages divided between the coast and the country, with its main part inland. Farming citrus fruits remains the major occupation here, with tourism still in its infancy. Should you want to visit Gundogan, stay on the *dolmus* instead of alighting outside the village, then walk back to the starting point for the walk indicated below.

Along any of our walks there is a reasonable chance of seeing a camel or a string of them. Camels have been used around the Bodrum peninsula as beasts of burden for many years. A fully-grown camel is capable of carrying a considerable load, which is useful to both the farmer and the populace in general. Camels move quietly and gracefully, and the sight of one loaded with a refrigerator, tables and chairs seems incongruous in view of their aristocratic demeanour. Camels are treated much as other domesticated farm animals: they are bred, reared and turned out unattended to graze, often in the phrygana. It is in this environment that you are most likely to see them while out walking, and the usual response from the camel is a stately head turned in curiosity. Tourism inevitably brings change, and the local people are now finding these intriguing animals useful for earning tourist revenue.

Alight from the *dolmus* just as it turns right off the main road to head into the village of Gundogan. There is no obvious point where you can ask the driver to stop, so watch out for an old, almost deserted village on the left, some 19 minutes from Bodrum, and prepare to leave the *dolmus* as it goes over the next rise. Ask the driver to stop at the second turning on the right (the first being a track). Then **start the walk** by crossing the main road opposite the junction, to find a trail which dips down from the road.

Follow it for a few moments as it heads to the left, parallel to the road, before swinging right to lead you into the countryside. Pine woods feature more strongly on this northern side of the peninsula, and one cloaks the hillside to the right. When the trail divides to pass either side of a well, in **5min**, the fork to the right is better underfoot.

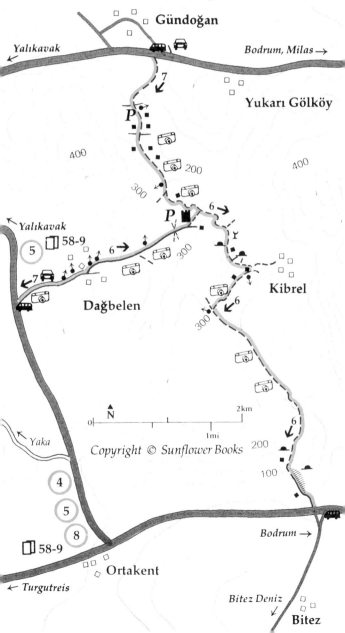

Continue in the ascent, enjoying some shade. Recently reconstructed sections of the trail, like the one reached in **9min**, suggest that this is an important route.

Cross a stream two minutes later, to aim just to the right of the ruined building ahead, which you pass in **12min**. Just before the ruin there is a lovely pine-shaded area, where you might be tempted to picnic. The ruin is surrounded by thickets of prickly pear cactus, but this is quickly exchanged for more open countryside as you continue along the trail. The many small valleys created by the folds in the hillside add interest to the route as the trail winds its way in and out of them to ascend the mountain. In **17min** you pass a house on the right and a stone tower on the left; a minute later, a stream bed is crossed.

It's now time to slow the pace a little, as you move into a steeper ascent along this sunken section of the trail. At a division in the path (**21min**), the left-hand fork offers easier walking, but just keep going upwards over the area of shale, to where the trail becomes more clearly defined again. Some cultivation is reached in **25min**, with a scatter of farm buildings; the trail weaves its way through them to divide briefly again just two minutes later. Looking backwards there are sweeping views down the hillside back to Gundogan. Ahead of you, the partly-shaded sunken trail continues in a steady ascent to reach the pine woods (**34min**). Soon pass a meadow on the left, and then a well on the right — just before a fork in the path (**36min**). Go left to continue around the top of the meadow (*yayla*), turning left a minute later at the top of it, to pass a house on the left. The path roughly follows the line of a wall on the left for a short time until, in **41min**, you swing sharp right. Looking back now, you can see ruins at the bottom of the *yayla* and, beyond it, the old village of Yukari Golkoy (which you passed on the *dolmus* just before alighting). Commanding views remain with you until you meet the junction with the Dagbelen trail in **45min**. Turn right on it (but keep straight on for the Alternative walk to the Bitez road).

From here you can easily carry on to Dagbelen, by following (in reverse) the notes for Walk 6 — from the 46min point (page 71). Stay on the main trail, ignoring the cross-paths encountered almost straight away, and keep straight on when a path forks off down to the left (**1h5min**). Head through the village when you reach it in **1h10min**, to join the track leading to the main road. There you can catch the *dolmus* returning from Yalikavak to Bodrum.

8 ORTAKENT • YAKA • DEREKOY

See map pages 58-59

Distance: 11.9km/7.4mi; 2h10min

Grade: moderate. The paths and tracks followed in this walk are not too bad underfoot, but there are some stony sections and some stiff uphill gradients beyond Yaka for a time — to an altitude of 275m/900ft.

Equipment: sturdy shoes or boots, long-sleeved shirt, long trousers, sunglasses, suncream, cardigan, raingear, picnic and water

How to get there: 🚐 *dolmus* to Ortakent (using the service from Bodrum to Ortakent, Turgutreis or Gumusluk), frequent departures (see timetable section). Journey time about 10min

To return: 🚐 *dolmus* back to Bodrum, using the return service from Gumusluk.

Short walks: There are two options for shortening the walk; both fall into the easy grade but require the same equipment.

1 Ortakent to Yaka (7.0km/4.4mi; 1h20min). Follow the notes for the main walk until you meet the track leading into Yaka in 47min. Turn right here but, a minute later (at the next junction of tracks), do not turn left, but keep straight on — heading below the village. Stay on this track, keeping straight ahead as you run into another track in less than 4min, to reach the main road some 25min later. Wait here to catch the *dolmus* returning from Yalikavak to Bodrum.

2 Ortakent—Yaka—Ortakent (8.5km/5.3mi; 1h40min). Follow the route of Short walk 8-1 above to reach Yaka and, similarly, keep straight on at the track junction reached in 48min. But after 3min, just before joining the next track, take the path downhill right. Use the notes for Walk 4 (from the 1h32min-point, page 65), to return to Ortakent.

A s you travel out by *dolmus* from Bodrum to the start of this walk, you may notice partly-constructed wooden boats by the roadside. Boat building is an old industry in these parts but has more recently adopted a new design, the *gulet*, taken from the Italian *gouletta* — a kind of schooner incorporating features from the Arab *baggala*. The hull has evolved considerably, as has the rigging, but the latter is now more for show, since the *gulet* is usually powered by a large diesel engine. It is an all-wooden boat constructed from local pine and is very popular with the charter industry because not only is it good looking, but it has large deck area. You might wonder how the boats are transported from the roadside where they are built down to the sea. If you are unlucky, you might just find out first hand! It is a slow process: greased

gulet

blocks, which are moved constantly from back to front, are used as a sledge. Given the narrow roads in Bodrum, it virtually stops the local traffic. There is plenty of the finished product on view along the waterside in Bodrum.

The walk itself offers plenty of contrast. We start off in a region green with cultivation, where trees sometimes arch over the path. We then head into a stark and barren landscape, before returning once again to cultivation. There is a variety of interesting wild flowers and shrubs along the way, including autumn-flowering cyclamen, two different kinds of wild lupins, and mandrakes, *Mandragora officinarum*, about which so many interesting tales are told (see Walk 9). Particularly eye-catching, especially in the spring, is the giant fennel, *Ferula communis*, with its spread of light green ferny foliage. It provides a delightful complement to other wild flowers nestling close to it, especially the anemones.

Ortakent, where you leave the *dolmus*, is an old village with interesting tower houses (see illustration page 63) and a row of ruined windmills on the barren hillside. If you have time, it is worth a few minutes looking around. **Start the walk** by turning into the walled-in trail on the right, at the point where you leave the *dolmus*. Straight away you can see Yaka on the hillside ahead, and our route will take you through Yaka and over the hillside behind it. Cross the junction of two dry stony river beds, to walk along the left-hand bank of the river to the right initially, and then along the river bed itself. When you reach a wall on the right, in **6min**, turn right into a walled-in trail. This brings you to a junction of trails by a house on the left within a minute. Turn left here, shortly to reach an open area with a pumping station (**10min**).

Here the trail divides; go left into a sunken walled-in path, where moss paints the rocks green, and the show of cyclamen foliage hints at the display of flowers to come in the autumn. When you reach the river bed, in **13min**, turn right onto the sandy path alongside it. Three minutes later you zig-zag across the river bed — so that it ends up on your right. Then, as the course of the river swings away to the right (**18min**), turn left up a smaller dry stream bed to rise onto a path on the right. Filtered sunlight dapples the path as you pass through a bower of trees, before the path leads away from the stream to join a walled-in trail (**21min**). The enclosing walls take a wider course around an area of bedrock, where you turn left (**23min**), going down a narrow walled-in path between the olive groves, with a stream on the right. You cross the stream two minutes later and move away from it. Greenness encloses this section of the path, with mossy rocks. Encroaching shrubs of holly oak and *Pistacia lentiscus* make passage a little difficult in parts — but it is a fairly well-used route, so there should be no problems. Turn right at the junction reached in **31min** and continue along a walled-in trail which leads gently up a ridge, enjoying some shade from olive trees lining the route. With the gain in altitude the views open up, and you can see some greenhouses down on the right (see below). Ignore the trail off left (**38min**), and keep straight uphill. Shortly you reach a rocky area, where the path breaks into smaller ways: keep left by the wall, until you find yourself back on a now-sunken path.

An open area and a track, reached in **47min**, signal the outskirts of Yaka; turn right here. On meeting another track a minute later, turn up left (but go straight on if you are doing Short walk 8-2 by joining up with Walk 4). Swing right with the track as it climbs above and around the village of Yaka, presenting good viewpoints along the way. Turn right at the junction with the next track (**53min**), to climb steeply above the village. As you swing sharply left four minutes later, you start to leave the village behind. The highest part of the walk is reached in **1h2min,** at the top of the hill between valleys: from here you can see a hilltop with a mast over to the left. Pine woods ahead promise shade as you follow the track into a descent (steep in parts) which passes through patches of phrygana where lavender, *Lavandula stoechas,* can be detected by its aromatic perfume, if not by its dark blue flowers.

Dominating the view now is an angular rocky summit

overlooking a fertile green valley sprinkled with red-roofed houses. Our way takes you down into the valley to reach the nearest of the houses, before taking a different direction to Derekoy. Ignore the track off left, at **1h11min**, and stay with the main track as it leads down towards the valley bottom to cross a stream bed before meeting a double gate (**1h17min**). Sometimes this gate is closed across the track: pass through and leave it as you find it. Close by, on the right, is the huge angular rock

Some 35min en route, the views open up, and you can see some greenhouses down to the right — these lie on the route of Short walk 8-2 and Walk 4.

which looks even more impressive from here. But keep your eyes to the left: in under two minutes you find the path heading towards the first of the red-roofed houses. Follow it to pass the front of the house, then turn left into a walled-in path starting immediately beyond the house. It heads down to the side of it and you pass through a gate almost straight away (**1h21min**). Enjoy the flavour of this lovely section of walled-in path, where oleander provides the colour and myrtle the scent.

You follow the course of the stream on the left. There is a feeder stream to cross, in **1h26min**, before the path leaves the course of the main stream two minutes later and heads for slightly higher ground. Down to your left citrus fruit and olive are farmed on the fertile land adjacent to the stream. Ignore the path joining from the left immediately beyond the frog-filled water trough (**1h42min**) and continue ahead to pass between a wall and a building. Then leave the cultivation behind for more sparse surroundings. The path dips down to cross a stream (**1h46min**), before meeting a rough walled-in track that joins on a bend: here you continue straight ahead. Along the way you can see a walled aqueduct built for irrigation. The way becomes cobbled (**1h56min**) for a minute, until you reach a stream bed a minute later. Then it is a very wide track leading to Derekoy. You emerge on the main road just below the village (**2h10min**). Either wait here for the *dolmus* to Bodrum, or turn right to visit Derekoy first.

9 AROUND AND ABOVE KONACIK

See map page 85

Distance: 15.2km/9.5mi; 3h20min

Grade: moderate-strenuous. This walk is mainly on (sometimes stony) footpaths, and there is a fair amount of uphill work, from sea level to an altitude of 500m/1650ft.

Equipment: sturdy shoes or boots, long-sleeved shirt, long trousers, sunglasses, suncream, cardigan, raingear, picnic and water

How to get there: 🚌 *dolmus* to Konacik using any westbound service (except Gumbet), frequent departures (see timetable section). Journey time 5min

To return: 🚌 *dolmus* from Konacik to Bodrum

Short walk: Try a ramble around Konacik (6.0km/3.75mi; 1h10min; easy; same equipment). This shortened version provides the opportunity to explore the interesting countryside around the old village of Konacik without too much exertion. Follow the notes for the main walk to reach the stony meadow in 34min; then return by the same route.

This walk heads into the wild interior of the peninsula, penetrating a beautiful valley before climbing out at the far end. Good viewpoints are the reward for your effort — as well as some unexpected old ruins which mark the turning point, before we head back the same way.

The sense of history is never too far away on the Bodrum peninsula, with flowers as well as ruins around to remind you of past cultures and civilisations. One such plant that you can expect to see on this walk is the mandrake, *Mandragora officinarum*, which was referred to back in biblical times and is associated with many legends. It is recognised by its flat rosette of large, wrinkled, dark green leaves, often achieving a spread up to 2ft across, bearing a cluster of short-stalked, usually blue flowers, in the spring, followed by large round berries. Many of the legends arise from the shape of the tap

Konacik, a very old, but still partly inhabited, hamlet

root, which is often forked and strongly likened to the human figure. It was believed to have powers of curing infertility or to act as a love potion. It was also said to shriek when pulled from the ground, and that this cry brought death to those who heard it. The mandrake had a place in medicine, too; both the roots and the leaves have been used in various treatments.

Ask the driver for Konacik, which is only a small place, but a regular stop on the *dolmus* run. **Start the walk** as you leave the *dolmus* by heading up the track inland and straight into the countryside. Ignore the track joining from the left in **3min** and continue ahead on the main track, to reach a fork in **9min**, where you keep right. A walled-in track leads you past a small hamlet over to the left, and you pass the track to it in **13min**. The way dips down, in **16min**, to join another track. Here you continue around to the left, passing a well (also on the left) and some interesting spring flowers like the pink butterfly orchid, *Orchis papilionacea*. As you reach a glade with a huge spreading olive tree, some two minutes later, look for the mandrake down on the right in the region of the well; there are some very large specimens which flower in shades of purple, with the occasional white one around.

The track leads through the old, but still inhabited hamlet of Konacik (photograph opposite) in **20min.** From here there are views down to the coast, before the track ends at a farm gate two minutes later. Here we join a trail which leads off to the left, but in **24min** we swing left onto a path — through a 'tunnel' of plants, where the dense-flowered orchid, *Neotinea maculata*, and the pretty anatolian orchid, *Orchis anatolica,* find a home. Ignore the small path off left (**28min**), and keep ahead on the stony path skirting the olive groves, to reach a fork four minutes later. Here keep up, on the path to the right. When you reach a stony meadow (**34min**), with huge mastic bushes in neatly-rounded mounds and ancient olive trees, the path becomes confused with animal tracks. Just continue ahead and a little to the right — heading for (and passing to the left of) an old olive tree whose trunk has divided into three parts. Then aim slightly left, towards the hillside immediately ahead (where a boundary wall mounts the rise) and pick up the stony path which leads up the hillside; keep the boundary wall on your left.

The path soon becomes more obvious and is easily followed as you climb to the top of this hillside (**39min**). Then keep right alongside a tree-lined valley, until you pass a steep cliff on the far side (**42min**). From here you drop down left to the richly-vegetated valley floor, where wild olive, strawberry trees (*Arbutus andrachne*), and Jerusalem sage (*Phlomis fruticosa*) sometimes crowd the path and hide flowers like the giant orchid, *Barlia robertiana*. The windmills on the Gumbet peninsula can be seen from here, if you spare a moment to look backwards. It may seem that there is no way out of the valley — but just keep pressing on. After **56min** the path starts to rise towards the head of the valley and, in **1h6min**, a cross-path is joined, where you go right. Take special note of this junction because it is easy to miss on the return; if you have any doubts make yourself an obvious marker. The path continues to lead you up and away from the valley for a short time until, in **1h8min**, you meet a major path.

The walk is completed by two diversions from here, before we return by the same route. First turn right and follow the well-defined path up round the head of the valley. You cross diagonally left, over a rocky area, to reach a water hole on the right (**1h20min**). From here take the path to the left, to reach a narrow saddle three minutes later. Both sides of the peninsula come into view from this vantage point, with Bodrum and the islands to the south and the mainland to the north. Retrace your steps back to the starting point of this diversion (**1h38min**), and now go straight ahead to explore some ruins. The first, which was possibly an old watchtower, is reached in **1h42min**. From here you enjoy superb views along the south coast. It's a tempting picnic spot, too, but there is not much shade. Continue along the path, past the ruins, heading into the pine woods. You catch glimpses of other, circular, ruins ahead, at a slightly lower level. These ruins (**1h55min**), although quite extensive, are at first masked by bushes; watch out for them on your right. The ruins mark the return point of the walk. Retrace your steps, to regain the junction at the head of the valley (**2h12min**), where you turn right. Look out for your own marker for the small path down left only two minutes later, and carry on (rather steeply) to the valley floor. Remember to leave the valley (**2h32min**) by climbing the path to the left, and take care, when you reach the olive groves (**2h38min**), to stay on the main path: it swings up over to the left (ignore the minor path running straight ahead). As you descend to the stony meadow (**2h41min**), head across it, bearing slightly right. At the far side descend slightly, to join the path leading off right, back to Konacik. Cross the main road to await a *dolmus*.

10 KONACIK • PEDESA • BODRUM

See photograph page 80

Distance: 11.3km/7mi; 2h35min

Grade: moderate. The walk is mainly on footpaths or trails, many of which are stony, and there is a small section to navigate without a clearly defined path. The old ruins at Pedesa mark the highest point at 350m/1150ft, but the short diversion to see the ruins requires a little scrambling and sure-footedness.

Equipment: sturdy shoes or boots, long-sleeved shirt, long trousers, sunglasses, suncream, cardigan, raingear, picnic and water

How to get there: 🚐 *dolmus* to Konacik using any westbound service (except Gumbet), frequent departures (see timetable section). Journey time 5min

To return: directly by foot to Bodrum centre

Alternative walk: Bodrum—Pedesa—Bodrum (12.6km/7.9mi; 3h; same grade and equipment). Avoid using any buses by walking directly from Bodrum to Pedesa, following the notes for the main walk (in reverse), and returning the same way. See town plan on the touring map to start.

P edesa is situated in the region once known, and still referred to by the local people, as Gokceler. It is one of the old Lelegian cities believed to date back to the sixth and fifth centuries BC, when it had greater power than neighbouring Halicarnassus. In the fourth century the people were forcibly incorporated by Mausolus into Halicarnassus, and the site was retained as an outpost. It is a fairly large site occupying a commanding position, but there have been no systematic excavations, nor any reconstruction. There are no roads leading to it; the only way to get there is on foot. So why not rebuild Pedesa in your own 'mind's eye', after enjoying this walk?

The ramble explores some of the interesting and quiet countryside behind Bodrum and returns from Pedesa by what was possibly the old route to Halicarnassus. Sound carries in the peace of the countryside, and the tinkling of bells from the animals can often be heard from distant hillsides. Somewhere along the way in this walk we heard the pure, sweet, clear voice of a girl break the calm morning air with melodious song — followed in harmonious duet by a shepherd. It was unbearably beautiful and stopped us in our tracks. We caught no sight of the singers, nor do we know the song, but we shall never forget the experience.

Leave the dolmus at Konacik and **start the walk** by following the notes for Walk 9 (page 80), to reach the stony meadow in **34min**. Head for the large olive tree with the trunk divided into three parts, but then turn right immediately *before* this tree. There are many goat tracks here, so you have to proceed for the next kilometre or so

83

without the guidance of a clearly-defined path. Head through the bushes to keep alongside the valley down on the right, and resist the temptation to descend for a little while yet. There are some interesting spring flowers to be found along this uncharted section, including the lovely mirror orchid, *Ophrys speculum*, and the yellow bee orchid, *Ophrys lutea ssp galilaea*. When you reach a rocky area, in **41min**, look for a path down to the valley floor and follow it, to cross the valley floor. (This is one of the very few places where it is convenient to do so.) Head up the opposite side of the valley, going diagonally to the left and finding your own path through the shrubs and bushes, until you reach some olive groves (**45min**). The way is easier here, as you continue with the valley on your left. In **47min** some ruins come into view ahead. The valley becomes insignificant as you near the head, and it is no more than a shallow dip as you cross it again two minutes later, heading for the ruins.

Whether these ruins (**52min**) are part of Pedesa we cannot say. Local information has it that this was on old Italian garrison with graves behind it — but we could not find them. When you have finished your own exploration, find the path behind the ruins; it leads almost immediately into a walled-in trail, where you turn right. In less than one minute, look for a gap in the stone wall on the left and go through it for a view of Pedesa lying on top of the nearby hill. It will be a bit of a scramble getting up to these ruins — only for the nimble and sure-footed. Before you continue from this point, look ahead and note the large rocky outcrop to the left of the walled-in trail; it is a useful landmark to guide you back to the path. Having turned left through the gap in the wall, cross a narrow field to the next wall, which is easily climbed. Then head towards the hill — keeping slightly to the right. It is another case of finding your own way from this point, using the small paths that take you up the hill through the bushes. It is a bit of a scramble, especially nearer the top but, once at Pedesa (**1h8min**), you can make your way carefully to the tower at the far end to enjoy the best views. From this vantage point you can appreciate the prominent situation of this site — occupying a position on a hill in the centre of the Bodrum peninsula, looking over the north shore just west of Torba and the south shore in the direction of Bitez.

Leave the ruins at the point where you entered them and return to the walled-in trail, reached in **1h23min** (use the rocky outcrop as a guide). As you enter the walled-in trail again, turn left and ignore another walled-in trail joining from the right a minute later. The route takes you skirting past the rocky outcrop and climbs away, giving good views of Pedesa. At the top of a rise reached in **1h29min**, you can see a small house ahead and to the left of the trail. It lies in our direction, but first the trail passes through a ruined hamlet. As the trail leads downhill, look for a wall on the right before the white house is reached, and turn right immediately past this wall (**1h32min**), following a small path running down alongside it. At the bottom of the field, two minutes later, ignore all the paths heading up to the left, and stay by the wall on the right until, in **1h36min**, the path leads away from the wall and towards the woods.

Penetrating shafts of sunlight sparkling on leaves and highlighting pendant grasses add a different texture to the

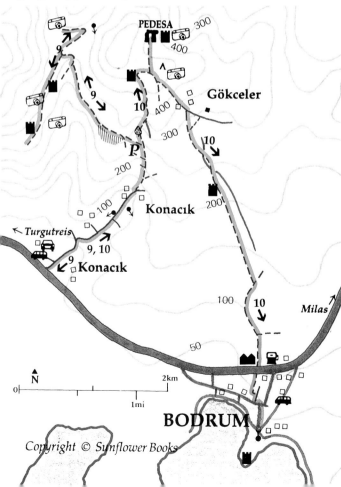

walk as you enter a delightful stretch of woodland, where the path is easily followed. On the left lies a valley, and our route keeps to the right of it, passing a number of ruins on the way — these may once have been fortifications along this old route to Pedesa. Bodrum comes into view as you round a bend and arrive at a junction of trails (**2h5min**).

Turn right to descend out of the woodland and towards the coast. A rocky outcrop is approached in **2h12min**; immediately beyond it is a fork. Keep to the lower trail, down right. You meet sections of the old walls of Halicarnassus as you wind down, finally passing through the walls by one of the old gates (**2h18min**). The now-sunken old trail emerges between a hotel and petrol station, to meet the Bodrum by-pass road (**2h22min**). Cross straight over here, taking great care on this busy section of road, and descend into a concrete culvert to continue into Bodrum centre. The culvert soon becomes a path winding through the olive groves. On coming to a T–junction (**2h26min**), turn right to continue between houses. Meet the mausoleum road (**2h30min**; turn right to visit it), where you turn left and then, immediately, right. You reach the square in the centre of Bodrum, near the main mosque and the place where the taxis assemble.

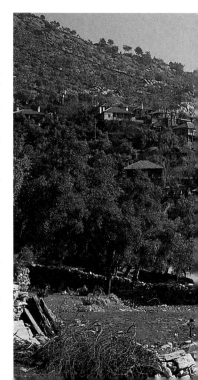

Walk 11, below Kargicak. Walk 11 is reached via Milas, and here is an idea for an additional foray: While there is little to see of the mausoleum in Bodrum, there is a scale replica in Milas. When you come by dolmus to Milas, leave the bus and turn right onto the main road. Turn right again almost immediately, to head into the town, with the bus station initially on your right. When the market is reached in some 15 minutes, take the next wide road up to the right (opposite the Turk Halk Bank), and a further seven minutes of uphill walking will bring you to the mausoleum, where there is a pleasant caretaker.

11 KARGICAK TO LABRANDA AND BACK (THE 'SACRED WAY')

Distance: 14km/8.75mi; 3h

Grade: moderate-strenuous. Only the distance, however, raises the grade, since this is mainly a walk along tracks. There is a fair amount of uphill work — to an elevation of 700m/2300ft.

Equipment: sturdy shoes or boots, long-sleeved shirt, long trousers, sunglasses, suncream, cardigan, raingear, picnic and water

How to get there: 🚌 First go by coach or *dolmus* from Bodrum to Milas, frequent departures (see timetable section). Journey time 50min. Then take a **taxi** for the 10km/6.25mi journey from Milas to Kargicak. *To return:* arrange for a **taxi** to meet you at Kargicak for the return journey to Milas; then return by 🚌 coach or *dolmus* to Bodrum.

Alternative walk: Labranda road—Kargicak—Labranda (20km/12.5mi; 4h, same grade and equipment). This alternative eliminates the need for a taxi. Ask the *dolmus* or coach driver from Bodrum for Labranda, and the bus will drop you just before the bus station in Milas, at the end of a road signposted 'Labranda'. Wait here for any *dolmus* turning down this road and again ask for Labranda. You will be taken a further 6km, to the next 'Labranda' sign, at a fork in the road. Start the walk by heading down the road to the right (signposted for Labranda). It leads you through well-tended olive groves towards the village of Kargicak, which is reached just after the surfaced road runs into track (34min). Follow the notes for the main walk from here, adjusting the timing accordingly. Return by the same route to the starting point, where you can either await a *dolmus* (although the frequency along this route is not known), chance getting a lift (as we did), or walk back to Milas.

Labranda, which is thought to take its name from the ancient Greek word *labrys*, meaning 'double axe', was not a city or a settlement, but a sanctuary dedicated to Zeus. It was joined to Milas, the nearest city, by a paved road known as the 'Sacred Way'. Built in heavy stone and stretching for some 12.8km/8mi, this has now been mostly covered over, but there is still a section to be seen near the village of Kargicak.

The location of Labranda, in the heart of the mountains, is delightful, offering distant views on a clear day. It is also remarkable in that the steep location had to be terraced to accommodate the buildings, making it an interesting site to wander around. The excavation work was done by Swedish archaeologists in the early part of this century, and there is much to see — including the remains of the temple dedicated to Zeus and two *androns*, or 'mens' rooms', thought to be used for banquets and other similar occasions. The First Andron is the most conspicuous building on the site, part of it still standing almost to its full height. The Second Andron, of similar design, was built by Mausolus.

Make an early start to avoid climbing in the midday heat — and be sure to carry plenty of water, since the track offers little shade, and it's a climb all the way to the site. Leave the taxi below Kargicak, just after the end of the surfaced road, and arrange to meet at the same place, allowing plenty of time. **Start the walk** by continuing in the same direction, passing below this lovely village and ignoring the track off right leading into it. Continue along the main track to pass through the cemetery (**4min**), which is on both sides of the road. Immediately beyond the cemetery turn right onto an old trail (the photograph on page 87 was taken at this point) which rejoins this track at a higher level. The old trail is probably the most recognisable part of the Sacred Way, and it skirts around the hill to the left and looks down upon a cultivated area to the right.

The trail rejoins the track in **19min**, where you turn right to continue in a steady ascent, enjoying a new panorama of distant hills in ridge formation and villages nestling into the hillsides, as if not wanting to be seen. The surrounding terrain is much harsher and more arid in this region, where a different kind of pine, with a lovely domed head — the umbrella or stone pine — becomes the dominant species in the sparse woodland. In **32min**, where the track swings left, you could make a short diversion (only taking a minute) to a pleasant glade — to rest or picnic: turn right

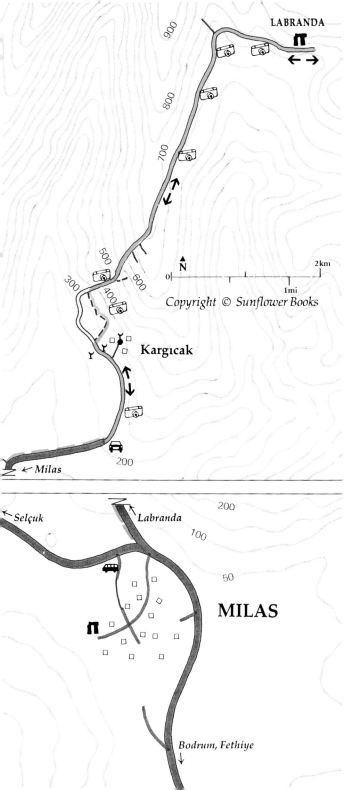

LABRANDA

900

800

700

500

300   600

400

2km

N

0   1mi

Copyright © Sunflower Books

Kargıcak

← Milas

200

Selçuk →   ↖ Labranda   200

100

50

MILAS

Bodrum, Fethiye
↓

off the track and head behind the large rock — just until you are out of sight of the track. Then return to the track to continue, and be sure to have sunglasses handy to counter the glare as you pass over the area of white bedrock. Keep ahead, in **43min**, and again, four minutes later, as tracks head off to the right. Rosy-pink granite and white bedrock paint the landscape in different hues as you approach the region peopled by bee-keepers, evidenced by the increasing number of beehives.

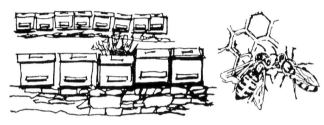

The first glimpse of Labranda is gained in **1h10min**, just as the track swings around to the left; from here you can see across the valley to ruins hidden amongst the pines and marked by some tall, graceful poplar trees. A junction comes up three minutes later, signposted 'Labranda'; continue as indicated along the main track to arrive at the site (**1h33min**). Turn left onto a path as you draw level with the ruins; it leads to a small gate, the unimposing entrance to this site. Enjoy the peaceful setting in the heart of the mountains and the wonderful views as you wander the ruins, before you return by the same route.

Walk 12 and Picnic 12b: From the saddle reached after 30 minutes, you have a splendid panorama down over Marmaris.

12 BELDIBI CIRCUIT

Distance: 10.8km/6.5mi; 2h   **See also town plan on the touring map**

Grade: easy-moderate. The walk uses a mixture of footpaths and tracks which are reasonably good underfoot. The climbing is limited to 200m/650ft.

Equipment: sturdy shoes or boots, long-sleeved shirt, long trousers, sunglasses, sunhat, suncream, cardigan, raingear, picnic and water

How to get there: No transport is required; the circuit is based on Marmaris.

Shorter walk: 5.5km/3.4mi; 1h; easy; same equipment. Use this walk just to see something of ancient Physcus and enjoy the fine views over Marmaris. Follow the notes for the main walk to reach the saddle in 30min and return the same way.

Marmaris now occupies the ancient site of Physcus, a dependency of Rhodes, but little remains of that era — only some walls dating back to the Hellenistic period. These are set on a hillside overlooking Marmaris, and we visit them en route. They are overgrown with shrubs, and it's difficult to get close to them, but the compensation for the effort required is the splendid view over Marmaris, by far the finest we found. From here the route of the walk takes an interesting course, as it follows the line of a ridge of mountains separating Beldibi and Armutalan. The path switches from side to side along the ridge, with constantly changing views, before dropping down to Beldibi.

Start the walk from the junction of the Datca *yolu* (road) and the Mugla *yolu*: follow the road towards Mugla. On coming to a fork in **6min**, keep left (towards Beldibi), but then turn off left, onto a side road (**13min**), just before the timber collection yard on the right. Ahead is the hill which hides ancient Physcus. The road through the flower-lined orange groves degenerates into a track, as you cross a bridge (**17min**). Shortly afterwards (**20min**), look for the path to the left, ascending a steep bank. Follow the path into a winding ascent and choose your own route as the path divides, only to rejoin again shortly. If brushwood is encountered along the path, then remove it to pass, but replace it carefully behind you. Stay on the main path in **23min**, where another path heads off to the right — and again, a minute later, when a small path leaves on the left.

Continue to climb away from Beldibi's valley, enjoying the shade of the trees and the lovely aroma of the summer-flowering myrtle. Keep ahead in **27min**, ignoring the small path off to the right, to reach a saddle three minutes later (see photograph opposite). From here you can enjoy a terrific panorama of Marmaris, the sea and the islands. Looking immediately left, you can see the huge blocks of stone that make up the remnants of the old Greek wall but, if you want to see more, then you must go to the far edge of the saddle and look left along the hillside. Although it looks possible to approach these ruins, in practice they are so overgrown with shrubs that they cannot be reached.

Leave the saddle by going towards the right from the point where you entered, to join a path (faint at the outset) leading to the right of a nearby rocky outcrop. The path

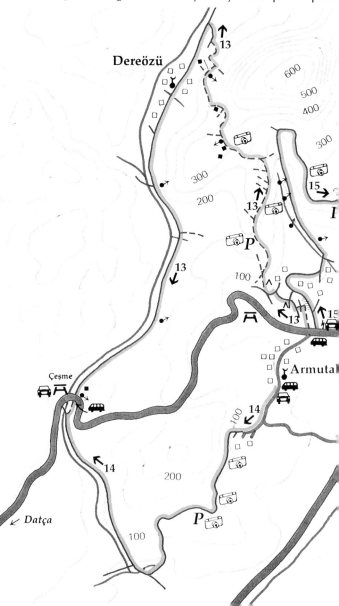

takes you out of sight of the sea straight away, and it becomes more distinct and easily followed — until you get to the next grassy area (**34min**). Keep up and around to the left, then go straight through the next grassy patch which follows immediately, to meet a brushwood fence bordering a meadow (*yayla*). Follow the fence up to the left. Looking back, in **36min**, you can savour a good view of the saddle and of Marmaris beyond. A slight descent

into a shallow valley follows; keep the fenced-in *yayla* on the right. You are now on a well-defined path. Looking up from here you can see the main Marmaris/Mugla road cut into the densely-wooded hillside. In **43min** follow the path first to the left, and then to the right, to skirt a *yayla*. Swing left three minutes later and make for the pylon on the saddle ahead (**48min**).

Turn right to continue along the saddle, taking a path which leads along the westerly side of the hill in front, so that you continue to overlook the valley leading down to Armutalan. The meadows are left behind now as you enter light woodlands of pine, wild olive, holly oak and the white-flowered *Styrax officinalis* — recognised by its deciduous bright green leaves, which are white and woolley underneath. Keep heading uphill, ignoring a path down to the left, and reach another grassy saddle (**56min**). The path crosses it diagonally, so that you continue on the eastern side of the next hill, overlooking Beldibi, to arrive at another small saddle just a minute later. If you enjoy peace and tranquillity for your picnic, then this is an ideal place, with some shade nearby and rocks to sit on.

From here the path continues directly up the centre of the ridge and, as you climb, you can look back on some fine views towards Marmaris. As you reach the top of the ridge, bear slightly right and join a grassy track which leads down to a main track (**1h2min**), where you turn right (Walk 15 joins here). From here back to Marmaris the way is all downhill. Keep a lookout down to the right: you will notice a minor track through the woodland below, and this is the route of the walk. Turn right onto this track when you reach the junction (**1h6min**). The track becomes rough, reduces to more of a trail, then shrinks to a path (**1h12min**), as you descend in the direction of a red-roofed farmhouse. Keep left at the fork (**1h 14min**), to reach the farmhouse two minutes later.

Head down into a cluster of farm buildings, to join a track, and turn left (with your back to Marmaris), passing through a gate across the track. The way soon swings around to the right and again heads in the direction of Marmaris. Meet a junction (**1h29min**), where you turn right to cross a stream. From here the track skirts the edge of the valley, with Beldibi over to the left. Stay on the track, to meet up with the surfaced road as you cross the bridge (**1h41min**). To return to the starting point, just retrace your steps along the first part of the outward journey, turning right as you join the main road into Marmaris.

13 ARMUTALAN • DEREOZU • *CESME* (DATCA *YOLU*)

Distance: 14.1km/8.8mi; 3h   **See map pages 92-93**

Grade: moderate. The outward route uses footpaths which are generally good (although stony in places); the return route uses good track. There is some climbing from near sea level to an altitude of 300m/990ft.

Equipment: sturdy shoes or boots, long-sleeved shirt, long trousers, sunhat, sunglasses, suncream, cardigan, raingear, picnic and water

How to get there: 🚌 *dolmus* from Marmaris to Armutalan, frequent departures (see timetable section). Journey time around 10min
To return: 🚌 any coach or *dolmus* returning to Marmaris

Shorter walk: from Armutalan to the high meadow and return (9.4km/5.9mi; 2h15min; same grade and equipment). The meadow (*yayla*), which is the highest point of the walk, makes a good focal point for a shortened version. Follow the notes for the main walk to reach it in 1h7min, and then return by the same route.

Longer walk: Combine this walk with Walk 14 (22.1km/13.8mi; 4h30min; moderate-strenuous; same equipment). The main walk finishes at the same point as Walk 14 so, if you wish to continue by walking back to Armutalan, simply cross the main road and descend the steep embankment to reach the track by the river. Follow the notes for Walk 14 (in reverse), to reach Armutalan, from where there is a frequent *dolmus* service back to Marmaris.

This walk has a certain sense of adventure, as you head deep into the hinterland, away from all traces of human habitation and civilisation — or so it seems.... Just as you convince yourself that there is no one for miles around, you come upon a beautiful grassy *yayla* (meadow), with its summer farmhouses and grazing animals. Dereozu, more of a scattered farming community than a traditional village, lies beyond the *yayla* and is the turning-round point of the walk.

A sea of pink and white cistus brightens the sometimes drab woodlands.

Walks 13, 14 and 15: The liquidambar tree is endemic to Rhodes and southwest Anatolia. Its leaves are quite similar to those of the plane tree, and it tends to occupy similar hibitats.

Much of the early part of the walk is through typically Mediterranean woodland. *Pinus brutia*, the Calabrian pine, is the dominant pine species, with undershrubs such as the eastern strawberry tree, *Arbutus andrachne* (its lovely orange-coloured trunk peels with age to an equally attractive cinnamon colour), prickly evergreen holly oak, and the ubiquitous pink and white *Cistus*. Amongst the less common species which occur is the Christ's thorn, *Paliurus spina-christi*, which is an extremely spiny shrub recognised by its flexible, zig-zag slender branches and small yellow flowers which form in the axils of the oval, minutely-toothed leaves. It flourishes in the hotter, drier parts of the Mediterranean. The 'speciality tree' of this region of Turkey, however, is the liquidambar tree (*Liquidambar orientalis*), shown above. You will see it towards the end of this walk, and on the routes of Walks 14 and 15 (you can read more about it on page 100).

The *dolmus* plies a circular route between Armutalan and Marmaris, either heading up the coast and returning via the Datca road or vice-versa. Leave the *dolmus* at the Armutalan/Datca junction. (This means that, if you head out along the Datca road, alight as soon as the *dolmus* indicates it will fork left off the main road; if going the other way, stay on until the *dolmus* has passed the mosque in the centre of Armutalan and then alight as the main Datca road is joined, 1km beyond the mosque.)

Start the walk as you leave the *dolmus* by crossing the main road to climb the stile over the barbed-wire fence. Follow the path going up the hillside, keeping slightly to the left, to head (after **3min**) briefly towards two white buildings. Stay below the buildings, and keep them on your left. The path is a bit vague at times, but head towards the right-hand base of the rocky outcrop above and beyond the buildings. Please mind you don't step on baby tortoises along this section! We found two here, so small that together they fitted into the palm of one hand. In **5min**, as you dip down over what was possibly an old track (now grassed over), continue on the path ahead, to join a rough track less than a minute later, where you turn right. There is a good panorama over Marmaris from here and, before you move off, look around for the Christ's thorn.

Almost immediately, as you crest the brow of a hill, you meet another track: cross straight over it, to continue on a grassy track. There is a confusion of old tracks in this area, but they are soon left behind. Turn left, in **9min**, as you reach a T-junction, and climb up to meet another very rough track a minute later, where you turn right. On reaching a grassy area (**12min**), where the track swings around to the left, take the path heading off to the right, along the line of a ridge. Down on the left now is the Datca *yolu* (road), and on the right is part of Armutalan (which straddles both sides of the Datca *yolu*). Immediately in front of you is a rocky outcrop which is negotiated on the left side, before the path returns you to the centre of the ridge. As you dip down to a crossing of paths (**14min**), go diagonally right, to continue on the right-hand flank of a hill. The direction here is due north, and the path cuts clearly through the phrygana towards a large carob tree (**17min**). Duck beneath its trailing branches towards the left, before swinging immediately straight uphill, to regain the ridge two minutes later.

There is a good viewpoint as you reach the high point of this ridge, but a more alluring place to rest and perhaps picnic is just as you descend from here, still on the ridge, to a grassy shaded area. Continue in the direction of the pine woods, keeping right (**22min**), and following the edge of the woods in a gradual ascent. In **31min** come to a fork in the path, where you head off right, taking the lower path into the woods. If you look around now, you can see that the route so far has swept around in a huge arc. Cross a ridge three minutes later, and you finally lose sight of Marmaris. Continue on the path, following the left flank of a hill through open woodland. Many of the trees and shrubs already mentioned can be seen in the following section of the walk. At the fork reached in **38min**, take the stony path to the right, from where you can look down onto a small *yayla* in the valley to the left. A sea of pink and white cistus brightens the sometimes drab woodlands (photograph page 95), before a pine tree cut for resin-collecting is reached (**44min**). The path suddenly looks less clear here, but pass to the left of the tree to continue through rocky outcrops and over another saddle. Keep ahead, in **46min**, ignoring the path which goes up to the right. Continue winding along the hillside at a fairly constant height for a time. The ground flora is never rich in this woodland area, but interesting flowers are almost always around, like the wild gladiolus and the purple limodore, *Limodorum abortivum* (recognised by its tall, leafless spikes of purple flowers).

As the ascent starts again, in just under **1h**, there is a rocky area to navigate, where the path is less distinct. Keep left at first and zig-zag towards the saddle; then follow the path around to the right and onto a rocky ridge, from where there are fine views. The top of this climb is soon reached and, in **1h7min**, you emerge with almost startling suddenness from the woods onto a beautiful *yayla*. Ahead you can catch glimpses of the sea and the cliffs on the far side of the Gulf of Gokova and, if you move a little to the left, you can see Marmaris Bay behind you.

There is a farmstead to the left of the *yayla* and a red-roofed house in the centre of it. Our way is directly across from the point where we enter, keeping just to the right of the red-roofed house and passing a well and a huge tree on the left. Find the start of the path which descends away from the *yayla* six minutes later and follow it back into the woodlands. (Ignore the small path heading off to the left two minutes later.) Rocky outcrops and rock faces seem to surround you at **1h20min**, and you have to clamber over some rocks. Looking ahead from here, you can see some red roofs at Dereozu. Stay on the main path, ignoring another path off left (**1h22min**), to climb to a saddle (**1h25min**), where you'll see a square windowless ruin, over-grown with trees.

The path leads down from here towards the cultivated region which makes up Dereozu, and the first evidence of settlement is a *yayla* reached in **1h32min**. Stay above the *yayla*, to continue through the woods on a path which is a little vague at first but soon becomes clear, as it leads towards a spring and a water channel. Keep uphill to the right, above the water channel; a house and a *yayla* are down to the left. There is a confusion of paths at this point, but continue on a path which leads towards a plantation of young pines. In **1h39min** you meet a junction of paths: here turn left towards the *yayla* — but only briefly. Follow the path as it swings around to the right, through an open rocky area, and descend to the right over stony ground, heading towards a fenced-in field. Turn right onto the track by the fenced field (**1h45min**), and follow it around the field (which is now on your left). Meet the main track (**1h48min**) and turn left onto it.

The leaves of the olive rustle in the breeze and glint in the sun, a stream gurgles on the right, and suddenly there is a different ambience and mood to the walk, as you wander along this track through the scattered farming community which makes up Dereozu. The mosque is passed in **1h59min** and, two minutes later, a stream crosses the track. The leafy shade and quiet tranquillity by the stream here beckon weary travellers to stop awhile to refresh themselves at this irresistible spot. This track leads all the way back to the Datca *yolu*, so you can relax from route-finding and enjoy the surroundings. Ignore the track joining from the right (**2h6min**) and keep straight ahead to reach a fountain (**2h18min**; again, ignore the track joining from the right here). Look for the lovely liquidambar trees, which border the stream on your right, and continue ahead until you arrive at the Datca *yolu* in **3h**. There is a fountain ('*cesme*') with good drinking water and also a café (open in season). Cross the road and wait on the Marmaris side of the bridge for a *dolmus* or coach back to Marmaris.

There are a number of trout farms around Marmaris where you can eat fresh trout in delightful surroundings. There is one in Cetibeli, on the Marmaris-to- Mugla main road, easily reached by *dolmus* (use the Mugla service). There are two more which are close together and lie just off the beaten track near Akyaka. These are easily reached on foot or by car. On foot, take the Mugla *dolmus* to Gokova and alight where the *dolmus* turns left at the junction with the Fethiye road. Follow the Mugla road for five minutes, to the bridge where the Akyaka road passes beneath it, and here descend the embankment to join the lower road. Continue ahead, with the sea on your left, and watch out for rock tombs on the right almost immediately. A further 15 minutes' walking should bring you to the first trout restaurant on the left, after passing a castle on the right, and to the second only two minutes later. Both are in beautiful settings, so it pays to look at both before deciding. By car head out of Marmaris to Mugla and continue directly across the Mugla/Fethiye road to re-enter the eucalyptus avenue shown on page 25. This road leads around to the left, to cross back under the main road and go on to Akyaka. Watch out for the trout restaurants very shortly, on the left. Off-the-road parking is available at the second one.

14 ARMUTALAN • *ORMAN YOLU* • *CESME* (DATCA *YOLU*)

See photograph page 96 and map pages 92-93

Distance: 8.0km/5mi; 1h25min

Grade: easy. The whole walk is on track which is fairly good underfoot, and there is only a little climbing involved.

Equipment: sturdy shoes or boots, long-sleeved shirt, long trousers, sunhat, sunglasses, suncream, cardigan, raingear, picnic and water

How to get there: 🚌 *dolmus* from Marmaris to Armutalan, frequent departures (see timetable section). Journey time about 10min
To return: 🚌 any coach or *dolmus* returning to Marmaris

This is a pleasing short walk which folllows a forestry track (*orman yolu*) through quiet countryside and offers fantastic views of Marmaris along the way. One special feature of the walk is the liquidambar tree, *Liquidambar orientalis* (see photograph page 96), which is endemic to Rhodes and southwest Anatolia. It is particularly common in the region around Marmaris and can be seen along many of the other walks in this area, as well as in Ataturk Parki just to the south of Marmaris (for more about this park, see pages 26 and 40). It is a member of the witch hazel family and is closely related to the American gum tree, *L styraciflua*. The name derives from 'liquid amber' and is a reference to the fragrant gum it produces, similar to the American gum tree, which is used in perfumery, as an expectorant, inhalant and a fumigant in the treatment of skin diseases. The tree can be recognised by the palmately-lobed leaves, not unlike those of the plane tree, although generally smaller. It does tend to occupy similar habitats to the plane, by streams and rivers, in ravines and on flood planes, but they are not commonly seen growing together.

Leave the *dolmus* at the mosque in the centre of Armutalan and **start the walk** by heading back towards the coast, which is to the right as you stand facing the mosque. At the fork in the road (**5min**), go right and ignore roads which lead off to the left (one minute and four minutes later). Already, as you gain height, there are good views back towards Marmaris and, as the road surface runs out and the houses are left behind, it becomes more of a woodland track. Stay with the main track as you round the bend (**12min**), to head up the side of a narrow tree-lined valley, where spring flowers add an interesting splash of colour. The red poppies take on a new luminosity as they catch the rays of the sun, which makes them stand out from the pink and white *Cistus* and the more sombre blue of the lavender, *Lavendula stoechas*.

After some steady climbing, another viewpoint is reached in **26min**, as you pass through a cutting to bring you momentarily onto a ridge with valleys on both sides. The views extend back over Marmaris and also take in Ketci Adasi and the end of Cennet Adasi, often referred to as 'Paradise Island'. The track continues to wind uphill, but the going is less steep as you approach the highest point of the walk, reached in **30min**. From here you can drink in the sweeping vista of Marmaris Bay and, if you want to linger awhile and perhaps picnic, there is some shade to be found by a large rocky outcrop.

Stay on the main track as you continue the walk into a more pastoral area, where cattle graze the spring grasses. A stream is met on the right in **40min**. Oleanders are very much at home by the water, and their lovely bright pink flowers garland the banks in summer. Notice the liquid-ambar trees on the right (**48min**); you will see many more along the rest of the walk. A track joins sharply from the left in **50min**; three minutes later the stream is crossed, as it changes course to join a river, now on the left. In **54min** a track leaves on the left to cross the river by a ford, but your way is straight ahead: keep the river on your left.

Woodlands start to enclose the track even more until, in **1h17min**, there is a clear division of eucalyptus on the

right and liquidambar on the left. Shortly afterwards (**1h20min**), the track swings left to ford the river and meet the main road. However, if there is too much water in the river, continue ahead along the bank to ascend diagonally and join the road after it bridges the river.

This is the same point at which Walk 13 emerges and, just across the road, you will find a café (open in season), a water fountain ('*cesme*') and a picnic area. Wait at the roadside at the point where you emerged for the coach or *dolmus* back to Marmaris, or return the same way.

See photograph page 96 and map pages 92-93

Distance: 13.5km/8.4mi; 2h30min

Grade: moderate. The walk is almost entirely on tracks which are fairly good underfoot, and the climbing is limited to about 210m/700ft.

Equipment: sturdy shoes or boots, long-sleeved shirt, long trousers, sunhat, sunglasses, suncream, cardigan, raingear, picnic and water

How to get there: 🚌 *dolmus* from Marmaris to Armutalan, frequent departures (see timetable section). Journey time around 10min
To return: The walk ends in Marmaris, at the junction with the Datca road.

Shorter walks: This walk joins Walk 12 and, when you meet that route, two possibilities present themselves; since they are of equal length, make your choice depending on your preference for walking on tracks or on paths. Both are the same grade as the main walk and require the same equipment.
1   11.6km/7.25mi; 2h10min. Follow the notes for the main walk to the 1h14min-point, where you meet up with Walk 12, and pick up the notes for that walk (from the 1h2min-point, see page 94) to return to Marmaris on *tracks*.
2   11.6km/7.25mi; 2h15min. Follow the notes for the main walk to the 1h14min-point, where you meet up with Walk 12, and pick up the notes for that walk (from the 1h2min-point, see page 94). Return to Marmaris using the notes for Walk 12, but in reverse. *Navigating in reverse requires extra care* on this walk, which takes you back on *footpaths*.

R osy-hued, pine-clad hills form a green mantle around Marmaris. This walk explores with ease this seemingly impenetrable barrier. The number of rivers and streams in the whole of this region came as a surprise to us — as did the waterfalls along the route of the walk, which passes through two distinct geological areas. The landscape in the early part of the ramble shows barely a trace of the imprint of man; there are no signs of cultivation and no great profusion of wild flowers. Wild flowers give a clue — indeed many clues as you learn to read them — to the infertile nature of the soil generated by the underlying serpentine rock. Serpentines cover large tracts of this peninsula, from the area to the north of Marmaris and westward, sweeping down the Datca peninsula. Although the area is extensive, it is not always exclusively serpentine, and pockets of fertility (associated mainly with the limestone series of rocks) do occur. Villages and

The Turks have the ability to squat and rest on their haunches very easily — and they do so often.

farming communities are few and far between in the serpentine region; usually regions of more fertile land of a different geology are cultivated. The high concentrations of metals like iron, magnesium, chrome and nickel from the serpentine render the soils infertile, and it is the high iron concentration that gives the rosy hue to the hills around Marmaris. Certain wild flowers are not only able to survive these soils, but actually flourish because of the lack of competition. The lovely cyclamen with the pro-peller-like flower, *Cyclamen trochopteranthum*, is one easily-recognised example of a flower which is only found on the serpentine soils in this region and, similarly, the liquidambar tree survives competition on this substrate. Should you find bee orchids or the evergreen *Cupressus* trees, then you have definitely wandered back into a limestone region … and you could be near the end of the walk.

The *dolmus* plies a circular route between Armutalan and Marmaris, either heading up the coast and returning via the Datca road or vice versa. Leave the *dolmus* at the Armutalan/Datca road junction. (This means that, if you depart Marmaris along the Datca road, alight as soon as the *dolmus* indicates it is about to fork left off the main road. If you come the other way, stay on until the *dolmus* has passed the mosque in the centre of Armutalan, then alight as the main Datca road is joined just 1km beyond the mosque.) **Start the walk** as you leave the *dolmus* by heading back towards Marmaris for two minutes and taking the track off left by the electricity substation. Armutalan lies mainly to the south side of the main road, but some of the outlying farms have spread north, and our route takes us through them as this walk gets underway.

The holy orchid, *Orchis sancta*, occupies a track-side position near the quarry which is passed in **6min**. Ignore the track heading off left (**10min**), and continue around to the right, to pass in front of a block of new apartments four minutes later. As you swing around to the left (in **19min**, where a track joins from the right), the direction of the walk becomes clearer, as you head through a small hamlet towards the wooded valley. A stream is crossed in **23min**, just after passing a white house on the right. A minute later another, minor track joins on a bend. Stay on the main track, heading up into the isolated valley. Masses of oleander paint the banks of the stream a cheerful pink down on your left and, all around, the tall yellow spikes of the mullein vie for attention.

The track starts to rise higher above the stream on the left, and there is the sound of water tripping over small waterfalls in **31min**. There are larger waterfalls ahead along this delightful woodland track, and you get your first view of them just before they are reached (**41min**). They are not so easily photographed, and you may need to scramble down off the track for a good angle. Liquid-ambar trees (see photograph page 96) add a splash of bright green by the water and confirm that this early part of the walk is taking you through a region of serpentine rock. More tripping waterfalls greet you and, in **53min**, you swing right into an ascending loop (ignore the track off to the left), to head back in the direction of the coast. Soon (**56min**) you can look down on your outward track and see the mountains and sea ahead, in the direction of Turunc.

The track leads you sharply left in **1h3min**, away from the main valley. You follow the left-hand side of a smaller valley, through beautiful woodlands and meadows. Walk 12 runs in to join this walk briefly, at the point where the track swings left (**1h14min**; see 'Shorter walks'). Our route stays on the main track, and we pass a rocky outcrop, to gain open views of Beldibi's valley below. The track heads north now, leading you away from Marmaris and keeping the Beldibi valley down on the right for quite some time. A small group of buildings is passed in **1h26min**, as the track weaves along the side of this lovely valley. Beyond these buildings, look for a path on your right marked with red dots (**1h39min**). Follow the waymarked path downhill and turn right at the junction of paths, still following the waymarks, to meet a lower track (**1h43min**). (Avoid the steep descent to the track here by diverting a short distance to the left, and turn right on joining the track.)

Marmaris is ahead now, and route-finding is fairly straightforward as you set out first for Beldibi. Stay with the main track, keeping right at the fork in **1h56min** and ignoring the track off to the left four minutes later. You reach the edge of the plain, where Beldibi is spread across the valley. The track joining from the right in **2h1min** is the route of Walk 12.

From here keep straight ahead, skirting the Beldibi valley, to meet the surfaced road as you cross the bridge (**2h13min**). Turn right on meeting the Beldibi road, reached four minutes later, and bear right again in **2h24min**, when you reach the Marmaris road. A further six minutes sees you back at the junction of the Marmaris/Datca roads, where the walk ends.

16 ICMELER TO TURUNC

See map page 110
Distance: 10km/6.25mi; 2h25min

Grade: strenuous. There is considerable climbing involved, from sea level to an altitude of around 425m/1400ft, in a fairly steep ascent. The walk is mainly on paths which are sometimes good, but often stony.

Equipment: sturdy shoes or boots, long-sleeved shirt, long trousers, sunhat, sunglasses, suncream, cardigan, raingear, swimming costume, picnic and water

How to get there: 🚌 *dolmus* from Marmaris to Icmeler, frequent departures (see timetable section). Journey time about 15min
To return: There are no regular services, but there are several options:
1   *dolmus* to Icmeler/Marmaris (only in season; departures uncertain);
2   water *dolmus* to Marmaris (only in season; enquire at the waterside café on arrival);
3   taxi to Icmeler and then *dolmus* to Marmaris.

T he route of this walk between Icmeler and Turunc is the most direct way between the villages and is probably a very old route. It is still used and kept open by the local womenfolk, who climb up almost daily to cut and gather branches from the strawberry trees. We had to find a place to stand aside as the women struggled past, bent under loads of branches. They stopped to chatter and explained that the cuttings are used as fodder for the cows. A nearby stabilised track follows an easier, but longer route to Turunc. Almost all the so-called 'roads' on this southern leg of the Marmaris peninsula are in fact stabilised tracks, and most are good. For clarity, we refer to the tracks used as main roads in this region as roads.

There is a straightforward division in this walk. The first part is constantly uphill, through delightful woodland that hides a host of interesting flowers, and the second part is steadily downhill with a bird's-eye view over Turunc. Some of the flowers to be seen on this walk include three endemic species unknown outside southwest Anatolia: *Cyclamen trochopteranthum* grows in profusion in places, but you can only see its propeller-like pink flowers in early spring; *Fritillaria sibthorpiana*, which is a lovely spring-flowering fritillary with a pendulous bell-shaped flower in bright buttercup yellow, is best identified by its broad, grey-green lower leaf; *Fritillaria forbesii* is named after the British botanist Edward Forbes, who discovered this species in 1842 (it is also a spring-flowering yellow fritillary, but one with very narrow leaves). There is yet a third yellow fritillary around, *F bithynica* — you may have seen before, if you have used *Landscapes of Samos.*

Start the walk as you leave the *dolmus* by heading up the road by the side of and to the left of the bus station. Turn left, **2min** later, opposite the school, to head along a narrow country lane in the direction of the old village of Icmeler. The road leads straight through the village, reached in **12min**, passing the mosque and a bread shop, both on the right, before emerging by a beautiful natural rock garden on the left. The towering rocks are decked in blue *Campanula.* Keep straight ahead, as you run into the main Icmeler/Turunc road on a bend, and follow it until the surface ends five minutes later by a café/bar on the right. The road continues as a track which swings away to the right, but here look out for the well-defined path off to the left and follow it.

The way is gently uphill at first, as least until you reach a clearing in **27min**. Woodlands soon close around the path and, immediately, *Fritillary sibthorpiana* graces the wayside with its dainty yellow nodding bells, as it does at

At about 40min into the walk: while the path is generally easily followed, the flowers in their variety vie for attention. White speedwell adorns the rocks and, with the colonies of Cyclamen trochopteranthum and orchids like the dense-flowered orchid, Neotinea maculata, all around, it is hard to make progress....

many stations along this climb. The path continues in a winding ascent, sometimes revealing views back down towards Icmeler (**37min**). While the path shown opposite is generally easy to follow, at some times you may be uncertain about the direction. In **50min**, for example, it heads sharply left, when the tendency is to continue straight ahead — but ahead there is no real path. After this sharp turn the ascent gets even steeper, and the path follows a zig-zag. Encroaching foliage from the storax, the strawberry trees, and the prickly holly oak sometimes obscures the bends on the path but, once you brush them aside, the way remains obvious.

At **1h2min** you approach a high point. This is a very stony area, like scree, and the path ascends in a zig-zag. The scree is soon crossed, and the way is easier going as you reach a more level area three minutes later. Continue as the path bears slightly right and then left, heading to the right of a white rock which stands about 2m high. Unusual amongst the flowers here is the white form of the orchid *Dactylorhiza romana*, normally found in shades of pink or yellow. At a small clearing, reached in **1h8min**, the path leads out to the left — although this is not obvious until you get underway. From here you start to climb a little more steeply again, keeping alongside a valley on the right, until a junction of paths is encountered in **1h15min**. Turn right here and continue on an almost-level path towards a valley scattered with large white rocky out-crops. Wild iris catch the eye along this undulating section of woodland path, which ends quite abruptly at a cutting. Here you meet a track (**1h23min**). Turn left to follow the track through the cutting, to an entirely different view-point over meadows and grazing cattle. Continue to descend along the track until you join the Bozburun road, in **1h31min**, where you turn left. Then stay ahead through the cutting a minute later, when the road to Bozburun swings away to the right.

There are fine views down over Turunc the moment you pass through the cutting. From here the road winds down through a series of extended loops, but there is also a path which descends more directly, crossing the road several times on the way down. Once through the cutting look on the left (in less than a minute) for the first part of the path, as the road swings away to the right. The path leads through woodland for a time, before rejoining the road in **1h43min**. Turn left and look for a continuation of the path (down to the right) almost immediately. It is a small shale path, which keeps above a concrete-roofed building and through olive groves. You again meet the road (**1h48min**), by a fountain. Cross directly over, to join a track, which starts off stony underfoot but soon becomes grassy. Continue directly ahead to enter a walled-in path (**1h 52min**), where the track swings right towards a building. The route skirts a graveyard on the right and gives good views down over Turunc. As you reach the buildings, in **1h57min**, turn right to join a track which leads down to the main road in under a minute. Turn left and follow the main road for a while, until you come to a sharp bend to the right (**2h5min**). Find the path which continues ahead off the left-hand side of the bend and descends to meet the road on a sweeping right-hand bend three minutes later. Here you don't really join the road, but keep across the corner, to continue along the path into the olive groves and then a fairly steep descent. Cross directly over the road, at **2h12min**, to reach the schoolyard two minutes later.

Here keep right and head down to join the road for the last time (**2h15min**). Turn right and descend into the village, passing the mosque in **2h20min**. Continue to the very end of the village (cross the stream and bear left). Here you will find a café at the sea's edge, where you can enquire about a water *dolmus* back to Marmaris.

Picnic 17 and Walk 17, Amos: Most impressive amongst the ruins is the small theatre which is outstanding not only because it still has many seats intact, but because of its beautiful situation. It is located on the northeast side of a hill, looking over a stretch of ultramarine water enclosed by a convoluted wooded shoreline which leads the eye directly to Marmaris.

See photograph opposite

Distance: 8km/5mi; 1h30min. Add time for exploring Amos.

Grade: easy. This is an almost-level walk along a track but, if you want to see the theatre, then prepare for a short scramble.

Equipment: sturdy shoes or boots, long-sleeved shirt, long trousers, sunhat, sunglasses, suncream, cardigan, raingear, swimming costume, picnic and water

How to get there: Getting to Turunc is not easy until the tourist season gets underway, then the options increase:
1 *dolmus* from Marmaris to Turunc. Enquire about departures. Journey time about 45min;
2 water *dolmus* from Marmaris to Turunc. Enquire along the sea front at Marmaris;
3 *dolmus* from Marmaris to Icmeler, then taxi for the 12km journey from Icmeler to Turunc. Note that the taxis usually charge more for journeys along unmetalled roads.
To return: from Turunc to Marmaris by one of the above options

S tarting from Turunc, this walk follows a coastal track which takes you a little deeper into the southern leg of the Marmaris peninsula and entertains you with some fine seascapes. The destination of the walk and the turning point is Amos. There are many ancient sites in the region of Marmaris — at least there are many marked on the tourist maps. The trouble is that the maps are not suffi-ciently accurate to lead you to them. Finding one is a challenge ... although Amos is relatively easy. The im-portance of this ancient settlement lay in its association with Rhodes and, from the style of the masonry, it is judged to be of the early Hellenistic period, with all the visible remains of the same date. Most impressive is the theatre, from where the photograph opposite was taken.

Start the walk from the mosque in the main street. Keep the mosque on your left, as you continue down the main street nearly to its end. In **2min** find a path on the left leading towards a rocky outcrop clustered with houses. Follow this path, climbing some steps on the right almost immediately. These lead to a small track, where you turn right. You meet a major track in **4min:** turn left. Now you can stride along and enjoy the surroundings, as route-finding is less demanding for a time. Hotel Turunc is approached in **15min**, but ignore the track down to it and look instead for glimpses of Marmaris through the trees, and views of the surrounding islands. Ahead, some huge sombre cliffs hide ruins on the top, which have their own history to tell — but these are not Amos.

The walk continues in a pleasing setting, following the edge of the cliffs, with the sea down on the left and added

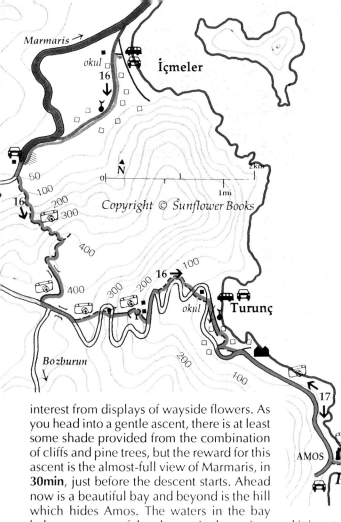

interest from displays of wayside flowers. As you head into a gentle ascent, there is at least some shade provided from the combination of cliffs and pine trees, but the reward for this ascent is the almost-full view of Marmaris, in **30min**, just before the descent starts. Ahead now is a beautiful bay and beyond is the hill which hides Amos. The waters in the bay below are some of the clearest in the region, and it is not unusual to see small boats here, bringing visitors just to admire the sparkling clarity of the sea.

As you reach the brow of the next hill, in **45min**, you can divert to explore Amos. Turn left and climb the wall at some suitable point, then carry on around to the right-hand side of the hill and follow a path up into the ruins. It is a bit of a scramble but, once on the top, continue until you reach the setting shown on page 108. Just before this theatre lies the site of the temple, but its deity is not known.

Return by the same route but, when you reach the Turunc Hotel, as you cross the track leading down to it (where the main track swings away to the left), take a path leading straight on, to cut off a loop in the track. Turn right on rejoining the track and continue back into Turunc.

18 ORHANIYE • CASTABUS • DATCA *YOLU*

Distance: 12.7km/8mi; 3h5min

Grade: moderate. Both tracks and trails are used, but the off-track walking is very stony underfoot. The final section follows a stream bed, and this part of the walk should *not* be attempted after a period of heavy rain. There is some climbing, from sea level to 300m/1000ft.

Equipment: sturdy shoes or boots, long-sleeved shirt, long trousers, sunhat, sunglasses, suncream, cardigan, raingear, picnic and water

How to get there: 🚐 *dolmus* from Marmaris to Orhaniye, but the service is infrequent so check times (see timetable section).
To return: 🚐 by coach using the Datca to Marmaris service (see timetable section) or any passing *dolmus*.

Alternative walks: These alternatives use different transport:
1 Use a hire car and park at the end of the track which leads up to Castabus. This is located on the left, just before the road starts to descend towards Orhaniye, and is reached some 5.3km after leaving the main Datca road. Pick up the notes for the main walk at 39min, to reach Castabus. Return to the car by the same route (4.0km/2.5mi; 50min).
2 Use a hire car and park at the end of the track leading to Castabus, as in (1) above. Pick up the notes for the main walk at the 39min-point and use them as far as the 2h13min-point (the stabilised track shown below). Turn left and follow this track to the car (8.4km/5.25mi; 2h).
3 Use a hire car and leave it in Orhaniye. Follow the notes for the main walk to Castabus; return by the same route (9.4km/5.9mi; 2h15min).
4 Use a hire car and leave it at Orhaniye. Follow the notes for the main walk to visit Castabus, and continue until the stabilised track shown below is reached (2h13min). Then turn left and follow the track back towards Orhaniye. When you reach the track leading off to Castabus, in 2h33min, continue straight ahead. The stabilised track swings right, as you pick up the old trail used on the outward journey and return to Orhaniye (14km/8.75mi; 3h15min).
5 Use the reliable Marmaris/Datca bus service (see timetable section) and alight at the junction with the Hisaronu road. Follow this road without deviation to reach the start of the Castabus track in 1h. Turn left onto the track and then pick up the notes for the main walk, joining it at the 39min-point. Follow the rest of the walk, which will take you back to the point where you started (15.0km/9.4mi; 3h15min).

A stabilised track is met in 2h13min, and then this lovely setting.

Many of the ancient ruins which are scattered around the Marmaris peninsula occupy settings which are outstanding in some respect — perhaps for their scenic beauty, or for their remoteness and impregnability. The sites always make an interesting highlight in any walk, and this is certainly true of Castabus, or Pazarlik, as it was once called. It stands at an elevation of some 300m/1000ft, in a deserted and remote spot on Mount Eren, to the south of Hisaronu. There is a temple and a theatre here (both 4th century BC), although little now remains of the theatre.

The sanctuary occupies a position on a ridge, where the temple of Hemithea stands on a platform built to accommodate it. Legend tells of two sisters, Molpadia and Parthenus, brought to this region by Apollo. Parthenus, by divine epiphany, received the name of Hemithea (half goddess). It was known as a place of healing, restoring desperate cases to health, and giving help to women in childbirth. Castabeia was the popular festival held periodically on the site, and this may have taken the form of a pilgrimage for healing the sick. A great fair was believed to follow the festival, and it is from this that the name Pazarlik derives — it means 'market'. Castabus flourished for some two hundred years, before it sank into obscurity. It is a little-known and unguarded site, where you can absorb the pervading sense of history in solitude — and feel quite restored afterwards from the exertion of getting there!

With the sea on your left, **start the walk** by the last hotel in Orhaniye, at the point where the track leaves the shore and heads inland. After **10min** take the second track on the right, reached just as the main track starts to rise, and continue through the cultivated valley, enjoying in spring the luminous display of poppies beneath the silvery-grey olive trees. Turn left onto a lesser track in **19min**. Almost immediately, it forks, but keep straight ahead, ignoring the path up to the right; you continue along a short section of what was once a walled-in path. You come onto track only two minutes later, and it soon becomes stony underfoot, as you start to ascend along the side of a valley. When you arrive at a huge carob tree on the right (**21min**), stay ahead on the stony trail; the track swings away to the left towards the stream. Loose stone, shale and bedrock make for slow walking now, as you continue uphill, passing to the left of the limestone boulder two minutes later.

In **26min** keep straight ahead when the trail divides, ignoring the steeper route off to the right (which is rejoined shortly), and enjoy good views back down the valley as you continue to climb. Turn off the trail to join a path on the right three minutes later; this brings you back to meet the trail in a further minute. From here the ascent steepens still more until, once over the steepest part (**34min**), the trail merges with another from the left. Pines provide some shade for a while, as you near the top of this section and, in **39min**, the trail joins a stabilised track (which serves as the road in these parts). Turn right on joining the 'road', and turn right again almost immediately, onto a stony track (this is the starting point for Alternative walks 18-1 and 18–2, and where you join in for Alternative walk 18-5).

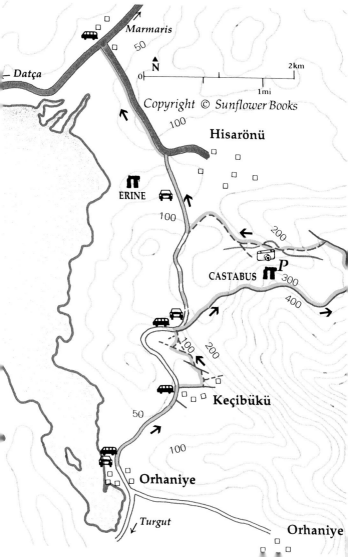

There is little shade to enjoy, apart from the occasional pine along the way, and the route is still uphill — but not rising as steeply as the first section. Tree heather, lavender and *Cistus* make up the wayside flora and, in parts, beehives line the route, as they do on many other walks. Looking ahead in **56min** the high mountain, Eren Dag, comes into view, framed by the pine-clad hills to the right. Soon after (**1h3min**), you reach a pine-shaded clearing with views down the valley to the sea — a pleasing place to stop for refreshments. Just a minute on from here, if you look down left, you can see the ancient theatre moulded into the hillside. It occupies a position with fine views down to the sea. Little of the theatre is now intact, but you can make out some of the seating and steps.

The way up to Castabus is reached when you arrive at the brow of the hill in **1h6min**. Turn left here, and head for the right-hand corner of the wall that you can see ahead, to find the path that leads up to the temple. The site needs to be reconstructed in the mind's eye, but the panoramic view is superb. The sweep of the bay that links the narrow western section of the Datca peninsula to the Marmaris peninsula draws the eye, as does the small hill near the bay which hides the ruins of Erine.

Return to the track in **1h10min** and turn left to continue. It is pleasant walking through the mountain tops, looking down on the lower pine-clad slopes; for the sharp-eyed, there is a chance to spot an unusual orchid along the way — the man orchid, *Aceras anthropophorum*. The track becomes grassy underfoot as you start to circle left (**1h 19min**) around a valley. At the fork reached in **1h29min**, head down to the left, into an olive grove, along a narrow track. It runs out almost immediately, by a bee-keeper's hut. From here descend diagonally left to the valley floor, to find a path (**1h35min**) alongside the stream. Follow the path in this deep-sided, narrow valley, then descend into the dry stream bed to continue (**1h42min**). It is very much a scramble at times, since the 'path' invariably returns to the stream bed. Notice the beautiful Judas trees lining the stream bed, at their most colourful in April.

Turn right when you meet a strong cross-path (**2h3min**) and ascend the steep wooded hillside. Soon (**2h11min**) you're descending — it's steep and slippery — to join a stabilised track below (**2h13min**; photograph page 111). Turn right here (but go left for Alternative walks 18-2 and 18-4) and follow this track back to the main Datca road (35 min away). Here you can await a coach or *dolmus*.

Distance: 13.4km/8.4mi; 2h30min

Grade: easy-moderate. The tracks and footpaths are generally good underfoot, except late in the walk. There may be a **danger of vertigo** for some on the section just beyond Kargi.

Equipment: sturdy shoes or boots, long-sleeved shirt, long trousers, sunhat, sunglasses, suncream, cardigan, raingear, swimming costume, picnic and water

How to get there: 🚌 coach from Marmaris to Datca, regular departures (see timetable section). Journey time 1h30min
To return: 🚌 coach to Marmaris

Short walk: Datca—Kargi—Datca (7.6km/4.75mi; 1h20min; easy; same equipment). Follow the main walk, but go only as far as Kargi and return the same way.

D atca is a delightful fishing village situated west of Marmaris about halfway along the peninsula. The coach journey provides spectacular scenery and is a memorable part of the day. Serpentine rock dominates much of the geology; consequently, there is virtually no cultivation. Pine forests cover the rolling hillsides: a wild and beautiful landscape, largely untouched by man. The first signs of habitation, as you approach Datca, mark the boundary between the serpentine and limestone regions.

The village of Datca is very picturesque, so you are sure to leave with some treasured photographs. But it is quite small — too small to keep you occupied for a full day. This walk has been designed to fill the time, to make the whole day a more enjoyable experience. It explores the region to the south of Datca, largely following the coastline, and it visits two lovely bays. Kargi is the first and the largest, where some of you might be content to spend the whole

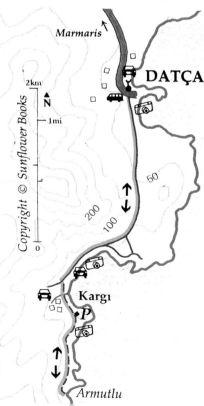

day. However, the second bay, Armutlu, has the intimate charm of seclusion and is well worth the extra effort to get there.

Start the walk at the bus station. Turn up the track on the right, opposite the mosque. It quickly leads away from the village into countryside and gives some of the best photographic viewpoints back towards Datca (as you can see below). In **14min** the track leads away from the shore

Photogenic Datca, from the track at the start of the walk

and cuts across the headland towards Kargi. It is hard to believe that the surrounding seemingly-arid and shrubby countryside could hide a wealth of interesting spring flowers but, if you keep your eyes to the right, you could expect to see a number of bee orchids — including the yellow bee orchid, *Ophrys lutea ssp galilaea* and the sombre bee orchid, *O fusca*. The small yellow *Gagea* species are everywhere and add plenty of ground colour, but look twice if you see a red anemone, for it may really be the red turban buttercup. They are similar in size and colour, so the only way to be certain is to inspect beneath the flower, to see if there are green sepals immediately below the petals; if so it is the buttercup, *Ranunculus asiaticus*. It has limited distribution, with the yellow and white forms only growing on Crete and the red form on Rhodes — and now near Datca.

As the brow of the hill is reached (**26min**), you begin your descent into Kargi, with the bay spread out before you like a map. Stay on the main track, to walk beside the shingle beach and the sparkling clear waters of the sea. Kargi is at present little more than a farming community enjoying a very fine location beside this enchanting bay, but it is surely destined for a role in tourism. Leave the track in **40min**, when it swings away from the shore. Continue along the shingle beach, crossing a small stream on a plank bridge. Pass Kargi Restaurant (**44min**), to reach the end of the beach a minute later; here follow the path around to the right, by the wall, and head inland. As you pass a small building on the left in under a minute, turn left, and then diagonally right, to climb a small hill, heading for the centre of the saddle (**51min**).

Crossing the saddle, you find a well-defined path leading through a boulder-strewn area, keeping just above the sea. The path becomes a little obscure in **55min**, as you cross an area of bedrock, but head upwards to find a clear path. Again, one minute later, you must climb a little to continue along the path. Care is needed in **58min**, where the path narrows on the steep-sided bank, and some walkers may find this section unnerving. The path meanders around the coastline, giving fine views — especially as you approach a cove (**1h6min**). The next cove looks particulary inviting, with the ultramarine sea lapping the shingle beach, and the path leads down to it in **1h15min**. This is Armutlu, a delightful place to relax and picnic, either in the sun or under the shade of the nearby trees.

Return the same way, allowing another 1h15min.

20 CETIBELI • CAMLI • CETIBELI

Distance: 10.5km/6.6mi; 2h25min

Grade: moderate-strenuous. Although no great heights are achieved, there is a tough ascent in the middle section of the walk, and the tracks used are often very stony underfoot.

Equipment: sturdy shoes or boots, long-sleeved shirt, long trousers, sunhat, sunglasses, suncream, cardigan, raingear, picnic and water

How to get there: 🚌 *dolmus* from Marmaris to Cetibeli, using either the Mugla or Fethiye services, frequent departures (see timetable section). Journey time 22min

To return: 🚌 any coach or dolmus returning to Marmaris

Short walks: There are two possibilities for easier walks, but both require the same equipment.
1   Cetibeli — Cetibeli (4.3km/2.7mi; 1h; easy). Follow the main walk to the point where the track approaches the farm gate (21min). Instead of taking the path off left, stay on the main track as it swings right. Keep right at the fork of tracks reached 3min later, and keep down right again at the next junction (30min). At this point you rejoin the main walk and can pick up those notes (the 1h55min-point), to get back to the main road.
2   Cetibeli to Camli (7.0km/4.4mi; 1h30min; easy-moderate). Follow the notes for the main walk until you emerge on the track above Camli in 55min. Then turn left, instead of right, and follow the track downhill, to join the stabilised track to Camli 3min later. Turn left here and walk back to the Marmaris road, to await the coach or *dolmus* to Marmaris.

V ariety adds the spice to this walk which explores some of the fascinating countryside between Cetibeli and the Gulf of Gokova. Natural woodlands, farmed acres, glimpses of old ruins, and wayside flora and fauna all contribute to the kaleidoscope of this ever-changing landscape. Wherever you find water, particularly slow moving or brackish water, keep an eye open for terrapins, which are commonly seen basking on stones or swimming about lazily — only to disappear as you approach. The chances are that somewhere along this walk, as along many of our walks, you'll pass beehives, too. Usually arranged in neat rows, the square boxes are seen in great numbers — possibly in the fields or orange groves, or even lining the track, especially in the pine woods. Unfortunately, they do not make useful reference points for walking notes, because they are constantly being moved around to follow the flowers in blossom. It seems that almost everybody around Marmaris keeps bees, a view that is reinforced by the number of shops in the town dedicated to selling the honey for which Marmaris is justly famous.*

*The local speciality is pine honey or *'cam bali'*, but this slipped down on our list of preferences when we tried some of the other varieties available. Perhaps top choice for us was the clear, sparkling orange honey (*'portakal bali'*), which is really made from *all* the citrus fruits grown in the region. Not far behind *portakal bali*, we ranked two others

At about 1h into the walk, the track leads above and around a cultivated plain on the left, where scattered farmsteads make up the village of Camli. Beehives line the track along this section, but they normally present no hazard to the walker.

Alight just as you enter Cetibeli, opposite the trout (*alabalik*) restaurant, and **start the walk** by crossing the road. Take the track which leads up by the left-hand side of the restaurant. Almost from the start, the way is uphill, through a peaceful setting, where small red-roofed farmsteads set in green fields create a pastoral atmosphere. Watch out for terrapins when you cross the stream (**7min**), and prepare to slow your pace, as the ascent steepens. The rich purple blossom of the Judas tree (one is seen in the photograph on page 127) shines out from the hillsides with all the gentle loveliness of spring, while neighbouring shrubs like myrtle and storax quietly await their turn to blossom. Another small stream across the path is forded in **16min**, and pines start to enclose the track.

At the point where the track approaches a farm gate, but swings to the right just before reaching it (**21min**), go towards the gate and take the path which leads up to the

from a seemingly less attractive source — cotton honey ('*pamuk bali*') and eucalyptus honey ('*okaliptus bali*'). If you want to try them all — and there are often small sample jars available for just this purpose — then don't miss out the flower honey ('*cicek bali*') or the thyme honey ('*kekik bali*').

left of it and skirts the meadow. (But stay on the track here for Short walk 20-1).

The woodlands which flank the path to the left are brightened in early spring by a display of blue and white *Anemone blanda*, with the lovely yellow *Fritillaria bithynica* also present, but in lesser numbers. Once beyond the *yayla* (meadow), the path heads more into the woodland and starts to descend a little, before a fork is reached in **28min**: keep down left, to reach an old olive grove almost immediately. Continue through the grove to pick up a woodland path again — this one a sunken 'tunnel', thanks to the surrounding shrubs (**31min**). You

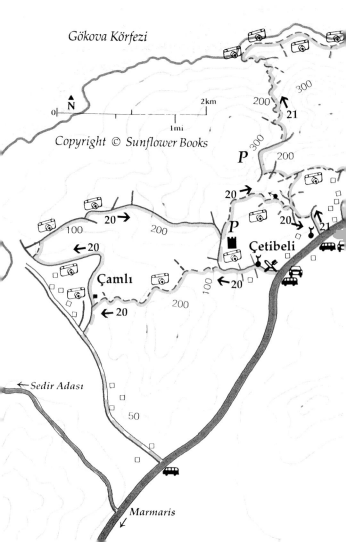

find yourself walking along the edge of a pine-covered valley falling away to the right, with the sea in view further over to the right. Take care in **36min**, where it looks as if the path continues ahead: it actually sweeps round to the right and continues to skirt the valley on the right.

When the charcoal burners are active in the nearby village of Camli, it is possible to catch the aroma even at this distance, as you start a steep descent (**50min**; take care on the slippery pine needles). At a fork, continue ahead towards a ruined building, ignoring the path off to the right. Pass the building a minute later and emerge on a track above the plain (**55min**; see photograph page 119).

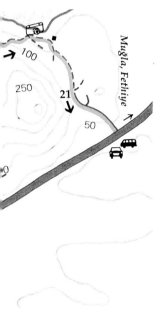

Turn right in the direction of the sea (but turn left for Short walk 20-2).

Continue as the track bends to the left (**1h1min**), but be sure to take the footpath leading up into the pine woods, when the track swings to the right (**1h 10min**). The path joins a somewhat vague and rough track in **1h14min**, where you turn right to continue uphill through sparse pine woods. As you descend into a hollow (**1h25min**), ignore the fork off to the right and continue on the track, to climb the hill ahead. The views open up as you ascend and, looking back, you can see the Sedir Adasi road, which is followed in Car Tour 7. Across the water, to the left, are the cliffs on the far side of the Gulf of Gokova. Follow the track as it continues to lead uphill, and stay on the main track when it sweeps to the right (**1h37min**), and another track joins from the left. You reach the highest part of the walk in **1h42min**.

Looking ahead to the shrub-covered hillside, it is possible to make out some ruins, including part of a wall and a doorway (**1h50min**). Several forts, both ancient and medieval, as well as some *amphora* factories, are recorded for this area; this may be one of the forts. (The *amphora*, shown on the next page, was a double-handled

vessel used by the Greeks and Romans as containers for carrying liquids.)

Turn right on meeting a junction of tracks in **1h53min** and, two minutes later, turn sharp left to join another track. It takes you below the hill with the ruins (Short walk 20-1 rejoins us here; Picnic 20). The track reduces to a path (**2h1min**) as you skirt to left of a meadow. In **2h8min** the path descends into the pine woods, to reach a water trough three minutes later. Shortly afterwards (**2h12min**), keep straight ahead to cross a stream, ignoring all paths both left and right. Continue along an intimate valley, with the stream on your right, and pass a huge plane tree on the right three minutes later. The Marmaris road soon comes into view and, as you swing left alongside a hill (**2h17min**), you see the red-roofed farms of Cetibeli. Turn right when you meet a track in **2h20min**, and continue across the cultivated plain to join the main Marmaris road by the mosque, where you wait for a coach or *dolmus* back to Marmaris. The coaches normally move fairly quickly along here, so be sure to give an early and clear signal if you wish to stop one.

Walk 21: This bay, with its shingle beach backed by an olive grove, is reached in 2h2min. In spite of its apparently remote location, this land is still farmed. The olives provide a valuable crop, which is gathered during the late autumn and winter months.

21 CETIBELI • *DENIZ* • MARMARIS ROAD

Distance: 12.4km/7.7mi; 3h   **See map pages 120-121**

Grade: moderate-strenuous. Much of the walk is along paths which are fairly good underfoot. However there is a steep descent down a stony trail to contend with, and two ascents — the first to an altitude of 300m/1000ft, the second somewhat less.

Equipment: sturdy shoes or boots, long-sleeved shirt, long trousers, sunhat, sunglasses, suncream, cardigan, raingear, picnic and water

How to get there: 🚐 *dolmus* to Cetibeli via Marmaris/Mugla service, frequent departures (see timetable section). Journey time 23min
To return: 🚐 any *dolmus* or coach returning to Marmaris

Alternative walk: Cetibeli—*deniz*—Cetibeli (11.7km/7.3mi; 2h47min; same grade; same equipment). Follow the notes for the main walk to reach the coast in 1h25min. Then return by the same route, until you reach the *yayla* (meadow) in 2h27min (this was the 23min-point in the outward journey). Instead of turning sharp right, keep ahead to continue along the path, with the *yayla* on your right. This soon leads you downhill in a zig-zag, to join a track 4min later. Turn left to follow the track, as it swings right on the edge of woodland. You come to a 'T' of tracks in 2h39min, where you turn right. The walk continues from here through a small farming community, to the main road just outside Cetibeli, where you can stop any passing coach or *dolmus*.

T he undiscovered shores of the Gulf of Gokova provide a spectacular setting for much of this walk, which penetrates a fairly remote region. Images of an azure-blue sea ('*deniz*') lapping a green shoreline indented by tiny

secluded bays linger in the mind long after the walk has been completed. In spite of all the isolation and remoteness, however, you are never far from farms of some kind along this walk — or indeed on most of the walks. Wherever there is land suitable for growing olives, regardless of the isolation or difficulty of access, then it is so planted. There is a classic example on this walk: having descended on a difficult but obviously-used stony path for a considerable time and through heavily-forested land, we arrived at the seashore to find … an olive grove.

Ask to leave the *dolmus* at the new mosque ('*yeni cami*'), which is located not far beyond the restaurant on the left as you enter Cetibeli. **Start the walk** as you leave the *dolmus* by crossing the road and taking the track on the right of the mosque; it heads directly for the hills. In **6min**, as the track bends away to the right, turn left onto a path which ascends fairly steeply into the pine woods. Almost immediately you enjoy views back over the fertile valley, to the pine-covered hills beyond it. The path describes a sharp right turn as you reach a narrow, tree-lined valley in **10min**. Go over a rocky area and come to a stream six minutes later. On crossing the stream you immediately meet a junction of paths: take the path to the right. It leads you back across the stream, and you continue along the edge of the woods. At a further fork (**18min**), keep uphill left, into the woods, passing a stand of American aloes, easily recognised by their huge rosettes of thick, succulent, spear-shaped leaves.

Turn sharp left at a junction reached in **23min** (the Alternative walk returns to this point), to follow a path up through the woods to another junction reached three minutes later, and here turn right alongside a well-fenced *yayla* (meadow). There is often a noisy dog on guard in the *yayla*, but it is soon left behind, as the path leads away and continues to ascend, to meet a track in **30min**. Stay on the path which continues across the track in a steady ascent, but watch out for the purple limodore, *Limodorum abortivum*, the curious saprophytic orchid which finds a home in this woodland habitat. Turn right as you emerge onto a rough, unused woodland track, in **34min**, and continue through the woods to a large grassy *yayla* five minutes later, where there is plenty of shade.

Follow the track as it leads into the *yayla* and then immediately swings right to lead you out again, back into woodland. The slender flower spikes of the man orchid, *Aceras anthropophorum*, are never very easy to spot, but when it grows in the middle of the track, as here, then it is hard not to see it. Each individual flower has the shape of a miniature helmeted man. Another *yayla* is reached in **43min**: here you head slightly right, to a path that you can see ahead. It becomes track as you set out along it. This little-used track is fairly overgrown, and it leads towards another *yayla* but, just before the *yayla* is reached (**44min**), take the path leading off to the left which skirts around the left side of this meadow.

The open area reached in **47min** marks the highest point of the walk, and from here the way descends fairly steeply to the seashore. Cross the open area, curving slightly left, towards the head of a valley, to find the path which starts the descent. Already there are glimpses of the azure-blue sea through pines and, beyond, the steep cliffs of the Gulf of Gokova. At a division in the path (**51min**), stay right, to follow the path as it leads across the top of the valley, on its right-hand side. The path drops more steeply, and care is required in places to negotiate the slippery pine needles lying on loose stones; otherwise, the path is good and takes on the appearance of an old trail as you descend further. In **1h6min**, where a tree blocks the way, continue ahead and avoid the temptation to go down left. From here the path becomes vague for a time, and macchie threatens to encroach but, a minute later, keep left when a path forks somewhat indistinctly off to the right. Footwork still demands concentration in this steady descent but, if you can spare a few sideways glances, the wayside flora has much of interest, including the spiny-leaved evergreen shrub, *Ruscus aculeatus* (butcher's broom), and bee orchids such as *Ophrys holoserica*. Ignore the path off right in **1h18min**, and descend to meet a cross-track a minute later, where you turn left to reach the bottom of the valley and enter an olive grove. The seashore is visible now through the olive trees and is reached in **1h25min**, by bearing right across the grove towards a ruin. A small shingle beach in quiet isolation, shade from olive trees, a vista of dark green wooded slopes sliding into turquoise blue, the smell of pine, and the sound of the sea combine to provide an irresistibly relaxing setting.

When you emerge from your reveries and are ready to continue the walk, set off with the sea on your left, to wind through the olive groves until you find the path. The path is indefinite at the start but stays at a low level, near the seashore, becoming more clearly established as you proceed. Wild olive and wild asparagus are present in the macchie which encloses the path, as is the ubiquitous holly oak. Now underway along this section, the path is easily followed, as it takes a line parallel to the seashore, dipping down occasionally to cross inlets. Ignore the path up to the right in **1h46min**; stay by the seashore, from where you can enjoy views of the Gulf of Gokova whenever the enclosing foliage permits.

As the path starts to rise away from the seashore, look for a fork, reached in **1h58min**, where you keep uphill right, to continue towards a bay which is now in sight ahead. This bay (**2h2min**), shown in the photograph on page 123, has a shingle beach backed by an olive grove. Skirt the bay along the shore, to pick up the path again at the far side two minutes later. The exit may be blocked by brushwood, but this is easily avoided by clambering over the rocks to the right. Follow the path as it heads briefly away from the shore, climbing a little — but still staying generally with the coastline. Once past the olive grove reached in **2h13min**, the macchie has been cut back more to clear the path and, from this slightly elevated position, you can see clearly Akyaka and Iskele at the head of the Gulf of Gokova. Descend to the left at the fork reached in **2h21min**, to head towards a bay which has signs of habitation in the form of a small farmhouse at the far side. Skirt the bay on reaching it seven minutes later, and turn right, to head inland when you come to the buildings, keeping to the right of them.

The next section of the walk takes you back from the coast, to rejoin the Marmaris road. Start by heading up the left-hand side of the valley directly ahead. Follow the path as it bears left through the citrus and olive groves, go through the orange grove wall, and then turn right to continue up the valley. Keep left at the fork (**2h30min**) and prepare for a steep ascent, when you have to tackle a couple of brushwood fences designed to keep the goats from straying too far. The path divides in **2h35min**, only to rejoin shortly (left is the shorter route). The going remains uphill for a time, but at least there is plenty of shade from the pines — until you reach an open area ten minutes later, where the path widens to more of a track. Soon the track levels out, as the valley is left behind. Now simply follow this track (ignore the track joining from the left in **2h52min**), as it skirts around a *yayla* on the right. You reach the main road in just **3h**. Wait here for any passing *dolmus* or coach back to Marmaris, and remember to give a very early, clear signal if you want a coach to stop.

22 AKCAPINAR TO GOKCE

Distance: 10km/6.25mi; 1h50min

Grade: easy. The walk mostly follows tracks which are fairly good underfoot, and there is only a little climbing — to 125m/400ft.

Equipment: sturdy shoes or boots, long-sleeved shirt, long trousers, sunhat, sunglasses, suncream, cardigan, raingear, picnic and water

How to get there: 🚌 *dolmus* from Marmaris to Akcapinar using the Marmaris/Mugla service, frequent departures (see timetable section). Journey time about 30min.

To return: 🚌 any *dolmus* or coach returning to Marmaris

Short walks: both are easy and require the same equipment as above.
1 Akapinar to Gokce (8.3km/5.2mi; 1h30min). Follow the notes for the main walk but, in 20min, take the track off to the right and start climbing. In 36min, just after a track has joined from the right (and where you can see a track junction ahead), take the path on the right — which simply cuts off the corner to emerge on a higher track 1min later. Turn right on this higher track to continue ascending through the pine woods. You meet cross-tracks in 43min: keep straight ahead, to pick up the notes for the main walk again (from the 1h3min-point).
2 Circular walk from Akcapinar (9.7km/6mi; 1h46min). This is particularly suitable for those with their own transport. Follow the notes for the main walk, to reach the cross-tracks on the brow of the hill in 1h3min. Turn right to continue downhill (the reverse of Short walk 1 above). As you approach the track junction in 1h9min, take the path down to the left — a short cut to the lower track. Turn left and continue downhill, to meet the track used on the outward leg (1h26min), where you turn left to head back to Akcapinar.

A great area of plain stretches eastward from the head of the Gulf of Gokova. Mountains rise all around it, but it is the foothills to the south which are the setting for this walk. The views over the green and cultivated plains make a pleasing contrast to the scenery on walks closer to Marmaris, and the bird life is different too. Particularly noticeable is the abundance of storks: they find plenty of

Some 30min into the walk, rural tranquility prevails, as the way takes you through citrus groves near Akcapinar. Farmsteads are dotted between the undulating hills, and a Judas tree is in flower on the left.

food on the swampy fields of the plain. This migratory bird becomes evident in springtime, particularly April and May, when on the nest. Storks are regarded by the local people as harbingers of good fortune, so their presence is encouraged, and their huge nests are never disturbed, even when built on top of chimney stacks. No matter where the nests are built, their size always makes them look incongruous but especially so when located on top of a telegraph pole....

Starting at Akcapinar and running in a direct line across the plain, crossing the main Mugla/ Fethiye road and continuing beyond it, is the magnificent avenue of eucalyptus trees shown on page 25. For the moment this 3-kilometre-long avenue carries the main road into Marmaris, but a new, wider road is under construction which by-passes the avenue and the small village of Akcapinar. While the coaches will use the new road when it is ready, it is likely that the *dolmus* will continue to serve the village. If you want to have a closer look at the eucalyptus avenue, then either make a short diversion from Akcapinar or stay on the *dolmus* until you reach the junction with the Fethiye road and walk back along it (remembering that part of it still carries steady traffic at present). The quietest part for photography is the section beyond the Fethiye road.

Leave the *dolmus* at Akcapinar. **Start the walk** where the main road bends (before the bridge) to enter the

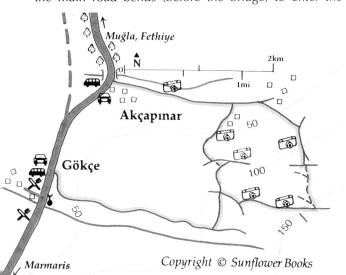

avenue of eucalyptus trees: head down a track between the houses on the right. Almost immediately there is a rural feel to the walk, with red-roofed houses dotting the hillside, citrus groves, and views of the green plain. As the track leads in a gentle ascent above the plain, it provides the opportunity for scanning for birds — the storks being easily spotted on account of their size. Ignore the track on the right (**20min**; but take it if you're doing Short walk 22-1). Take the right-hand fork at the junction of tracks two minutes later. In **30min**, at a fork in the track, go right and continue uphill towards the woods. You come to another fork in **34min**, where again you go right, but this time on a lesser track. This leads to a 'T' of tracks a minute later: cross directly over, to join a path and continue climbing into the woods, turning left at the path junction in **36min**. Continue as the path weaves uphill through the woods, to emerge onto a track in **49min**, where you turn right. The path does continue across the track, but only into a *yayla* (meadow), which is a pleasant place to picnic. Otherwise continue along the high-level woodland track, enjoying panoramic views over the plain. Reach a crossing of tracks on the brow of a hill (**1h3min**), where you turn left into woodland (but head down right for Short walk 22-2).

Grey-green leaves, that rustle in the wind and sparkle silver in the sun, announce yet more olive trees — this time buried deep in the pine woods. At the junction of tracks reached in **1h10min**, turn right. From here you can catch glimpses of the red-roofed houses of Gokce through the light pine woods. Nearer at hand are masses of the small, white *Gagea graeca* which grows so freely in the dry stony areas and is seen at its best in April. Looking down left through the woodland, you can see a river in the valley bottom and, gradually, the views open to reveal more of Gokce and the main road. An open area, reached in **1h29min**, is an inviting place for a break, especially when the surrounding spiny shrub, Christ's thorn (*Paliurus spina-christi*), takes on a yellow hue from a mass of small flowers in May. Stay on the track as it swings to the right and then runs parallel to the main road below you. Starting to descend, you enjoy good viewpoints over well-ordered citrus groves and towards the Gulf of Gokova. Turn left into Gokce, in **1h43min**, as you emerge onto the main road. Any *dolmus* or coach heading back to Marmaris can be stopped here, although you may prefer to walk a further seven minutes into the village centre, where there is a shop and restaurants.

23 MARMARIS WATERFALLS

See map pages 92-93 and town plan; see photograph page 26

Distance: 5km/3.1mi; 1h

Grade: easy. Some nimbleness is required to cross the rivers, and some short sections of path are difficult underfoot.

Equipment: sturdy shoes or boots, long-sleeved shirt, sunhat, sunglasses, suncream, cardigan, raingear, picnic and water

How to get there: No transport is required for this circular walk based on Marmaris.

C lose to town, the waterfalls (*selalesi*) visited on this walk are a favourite picnic setting for the more energetic members of the local populace. The Turks are great picnickers, but when it comes to eating, bread (*ekmek*) is an essential element of any meal, and it is often said about them that food is something to accompany bread. Try our recipe for olive bread on the next page!

Start the walk at the junction of the Datca and Mugla roads, by heading out of Marmaris towards Mugla, to reach the by-pass joining from the right in **10min**. Turn right into it and, a minute later (immediately before the vehicle depot on the left), turn left onto a track which skirts the boundary of the depot. If you tread quietly here, you might catch a glimpse of the terrapins in the stream on the right as you approach but, once disturbed, they are away into the murkier parts. The way now takes you up the valley which lies ahead but first, in **15min**, you must step over a broken-down barbed wire fence. Follow the woodland track beyond it, with a water channel on the left. You reach the first waterfalls in **17min**. Dappled sunlight, leafy shade, gurgling water and an old mill lend charm to this natural beauty spot.

Cross the river to the right by the stepping stones, to join the path at the far side; then head momentarily away from the river to meet an old trail (**19min**). Turn left to continue through the open woodland. There is a short diversion to a lovely picnic spot in **23min**: leave the trail and take a not-very-obvious path along the edge of a wall, towards a ruined building (reached in a minute). It is peacefully located overlooking a shady glade and a pool in the river (see photograph page 26). Return to the main trail and, as you continue uphill, notice almost immediately the small path joining from the right; this will be your return route. When you meet a wall supporting an aqueduct in **27min**, take care to follow the path swinging sharp right along a water channel. Down left, the river falls away over tiny waterfalls, but our path maintains a level course and meets the river a little further upstream (**30min**). This is another natural beauty spot where the pools in the river attract keen swimmers.

Cross the river diagonally, using the boulders, and continue to follow the river upstream, by making your way along the path that wends between the rocks. Just before the left-hand bend in the river, the path cuts a corner by heading up the bank and down again to the river's edge (**33min**). Cross the river, using available stones, and go up the path opposite, moving away from the river and leaving behind the shade of the pines for open macchie. Marmaris comes briefly into view as you crest the hill in **35min** and start to descend on a dusty stony path, which requires careful footwork. The outward trail is rejoined in **38min**; here you turn left to retrace your way back to Marmaris.

The bakeries in Turkey offer a good selection of bread in different shapes and textures, but for snacks the bread rings are more popular. Consumed in great quantity is the *simit*, a sesame seed-covered bread ring sold everywhere by street vendors, particularly around the bus stations. Also popular is the golden, honey-covered ring called *burma*, which is quite delicious and not as sweet as you might expect — since a crispy outside stops the honey from soaking in. If we are not buying the sweet bread ring, *acma*, then our own favourite is home-made olive bread, *zeytin ekmek*, which we first sampled when invited to eat with a Turkish family. Such was our obvious delight that we came away clutching the remains of the loaf as well as the recipe. It is easily made by mixing thoroughly 4 eggs, 125ml olive oil (bring some home from Turkey), 125g natural yoghurt, 1/4 tsp dried mint, the juice of 1/2 lemon, and a pinch of salt. Into this fold 450g self-raising flour and 150g of stoned chopped olives, to make a stiff mix which is baked in a 9in square tin at 190 °C for 35-40 minutes. This bread is delicious eaten with or without butter.

BUS TIMETABLES

The public transport system consists of the *dolmus* for short (and sometimes intermediate) journeys and the coaches for the longer distances. You may need to use both of these systems, so they are discussed separately below.

Dolmuş

The *dolmus* is simply a mini-bus, usually seating around fourteen people, but it can be larger. They mostly get filled to capacity and, when full, small stools are often produced to seat a few more. Standing is not allowed, but this is universally ignored. Smoking is not allowed either on many of the *dolmus*, but this often depends on the attitude of the driver. (However, non-smokers should not find fumes a problem in the summer months, when the windows are fully open and the ventilation good.)

There is **no numbering system** for the *dolmus* so, to find the one that you want, look for the sign hanging in the front window: it states the destination and, occasionally, intermediate stops. **Payment** is made to the driver on the bus, usually as you alight; and don't expect to get a ticket. Fares are sometimes passed down the *dolmus* to the driver, so you may find yourself part of the chain. The *dolmus* are very flexible, in that they will stop virtually anywhere on request for passengers to board or alight — and they will even divert from the normal route to deliver home somebody loaded with too much to carry, for a small extra fee, of course. **Timetables** don't exist.

There is some variation in the operating methods and organisation of the services in different regions. These are discussed below, separately, for Bodrum and Marmaris.

Bodrum: There is a well-organised, centrally-located bus station for both the *dolmus* and the coaches; it is shown on the Bodrum town plan on the touring map. The *dolmus* use the north side of the station, but there will be plenty of people around asking your destination as you enter, so you will be quickly directed to the right place. At the station office, by the entrance, is a board listing the *dolmus* destinations and prices, both for a single journey and for the private hire of the *dolmus* for that journey. Turkey has high inflation at present, which means that prices are increased periodically and, while the board is regularly updated, it does sometimes lag behind.

The frequency of departures of the *dolmus* depends entirely on the number of people travelling. Generally, the *dolmus* driver is unhappy to start off unless he has between ten and twelve people on board. At peak travelling time, or for popular destinations, like Turgutreis, then the *dolmus* fill quickly and depart frequently. Otherwise you must wait patiently until the *dolmus* has the required number of people, which can sometimes mean a wait of around 30 minutes, especially early in the season. There is another option if you are not keen to wait. If you are prepared to pay the fare for all the remaining empty seats, then the driver will depart immediately....

Marmaris: Since there are fewer surrounding villages, the *dolmus* system is less well organised than at Bodrum. There is no *dolmus* station as such; the various roadside departure points are marked on the Marmaris town plan on the touring map. Briefly, the Icmeler and Armutalan *dolmus* depart from just west of the Ataturk statue on the seafront; the Mugla *dolmus* departs by the school at the corner of Mustafa Kemal Caddesi; other villages are served by *dolmus* starting opposite the Ataturk statue. This is the situation at present, but a new bus station is under construction in Marmaris, which may eventually lead to some reorganisation of the *dolmus.*

The only frequent *dolmus* services are those to Mugla, Icmeler and Armutalan. The other services tend to arrive from the outlying village in the morning and return in the afternoon. They do, however, respond to demand and, when there are more visitors around in high summer, the services are more frequent. The **post buses** present another option for getting out to some of the surrounding villages. Although essentially for carrying the post, these yellow buses do carry fare-paying passengers. They tend to depart very early in the morning from outside the post office; enquire locally for destinations and times.

Coaches

These run the long-distance routes connecting Bodrum and Marmaris with all the major towns in Turkey, and generally they offer a good standard of comfort. The coaches operate from a station, *otogar*, in both Bodrum and Marmaris, and their locations are marked on the town plans on the touring map. There are a number of separate companies operating coaches in competition over the same routes. Pamukkale, Kamil Koc, Karadeveci and Aydin Turizm are just some of the companies, and you will see their names displayed on the side of their buses. Each company has its own ticket office in the bus station and some have additional offices in the town.

The system can be a little confusing for the unwary traveller. Each bus company has its own ticket touts and, the moment you enter the bus station, they descend on you wanting to know your destination. If their company has a bus going your way, they will quickly guide you into their ticket office and get you booked in. Don't let yourself be hustled; there may be a more suitable departure time for you with another company. Check them all first. When you finally book (and you can book in advance), your ticket will have a seat number, where you will be expected to sit. If you join in mid-journey, payment is made to the conductor on the bus.

Services operate seven days a week all year round with more frequent departures in summer. A selection of useful timetables is given below, but always remember to check your times first-hand. The name of the operating company is given in brackets. *Except for Marmaris-Datca, only outward times are available, but the return buses are generally of a similar frequency.*

From Bodrum

Timetable 1: Bodrum to Izmir (Karadeveci) for Ephesus
Depart Bodrum: 03.30 and then hourly until18.30; 00.30
Leave the bus at Selcuk for Ephesus.

Timetable 2: Bodrum to Marmaris (Pamukkale)
Depart Bodrum: 08.30; 09.45; 11.00; 14.15

Timetable 3: Bodrum to Marmaris (Karadeveci)
Depart Bodrum: 08.00; 09.15; 10.30; 11.45; 12.45; 13.45; 14.30

Timetable 4: Bodrum to Fethiye (Pamukkale)
Depart Bodrum 10.30

From Marmaris

Timetable 5: Marmaris to Datca (Pamukkale)
Depart Marmaris: 08.30; 09.00; 12.30; 16.00; 16.30; 18.30
Depart Datca: 06.00; 08.00; 08.45; 11.00; 13.30; 16.00; 18.00

Timetable 6: Marmaris to Fethiye (Kamil Koc)
Depart Marmaris: 09.30; 12.30; 14.30; 16.00

Timetable 7: Marmaris to Fethiye (Pamukkale) for Dalyan
Depart Marmaris: 08.00; then hourly until 16.00
Leave the bus at Ortaca and take a dolmus from there to Dalyan.

Timetable 8: Marmaris to Denizli (Kamil Koc) for Pamukkale
Depart Marmaris: 14.30; 16.30; 18.30; 19.30
Catch the dolmus from outside the bus station for the short journey from Denizli to Pamukkale.

Timetable 9: Marmaris to Denizli (Pamukkale) for Pamukkale
Depart Marmaris: 08.00; 17.30; 18.00; 20.00; 21.00
See notes to timetable 8.

Timetable 10: Marmaris to Izmir (Pamukkale) for Ephesus
Depart Marmaris: 05.15; 06.00 then hourly until 22.00
Leave the bus at Selcuk for Ephesus.

☀ Index

Geographical names only are included here; for non-geographical entries, see Contents, page 3. A page number in italic type indicates a map reference; a page number in bold face type indicates a photograph or drawing. Both may be in addition to a text reference on the same page.

Akçaalan (**Ak**-chah-ah-lan) 10, **49**, 50, *51*

Akçapinar (**Ak**-chah-peen-ahr) **25**, 34, 38, **127**, *128*

Akköy (**Ak**-keuy) 23

Akyaka (**Ak**-yaka) 99, 126

Akyarlar (**Ak**-yahr-lahr) 10, 16, 43, 49, *51*, 52

Alabanda (**Ala**-banda) 24-6

Alinda (**Al**-eenda) 24, 26

Altınkum (**Al**-tuhn-koom) 23

Amos (**Am**-moss) 12, **108**, 109, *110*

Antalya (**An**-talya) 35-7

Aphrodisias (**Afroh**-dees-eeass) **28**, 29-30, 39

Armutalan (**Ahr**-moot-al-lan) 12, 32, 91, *92*, 95, 100, 102-3, *133*

Armutlu (**Ahr**-moot-loo) *115*, 117

Atatürk Parkı (**Ata**-teuwrk **Par**-kuh) **26**, 40, *93*

Atburgazı (**At**-bur-gazuh) 23

Aydın (**I**-duhn) 28, 30, 38-9

Bafa, Lake (**Ba**-fa) 15, **20**, 21-3, 38-9

Balat (**Ba**-lat) 23

Beldibi (**Bel**-dee-bee) 34, 91, *93*, 102-3

Bitez (**Bee**-tez) 69, 72-3, *74*, 75

Bodrum (**Bod**-room) 7-9, 15-17, 19, 20, 23, 24, 26-8, 29, 40-1, 43, 62, 65, 72, 75-6, 83, *85*, 86, 132-3, 134

  town plan *see touring map*

Bucak (**Boo**-jak) 21

Çamlı (**Cham**-luh) 34, 118, **119**, *120*, 121

Çamlıca (**Cham**-luh-ja) 28

Çamlık (**Cham**-luhk) 19, 27

Çaniçi (**Chan**-eechee) 21

Castabus (Castabeia) (**Casta**-boos) 12, 111-12, *113*, 114

Caunos (**Caw**-noss) **17**, 35

Cedreae (**Seed**-ree) 35

Cennet Adası (**Jen**-net **Ad**-da-suh) 101

Çeşme (**Chesh**-meh) *92*

Çetibeli (**Che**-tee-bel-lee) 12, 34, 99, 118-19, *120*, 122-4

Cindya (**Seend**-ya) 20

Çine (**Cheen**-eh) 25-6, 31, 38-9

Çine Çayı (gorge) (**Cheen**-eh **Chie**-uh) 24-5, 31, 38-9

Çömlekçi (**Chewm**-lek-chee) 16, 19

Cumalı (**Joom**-al-uh) 33

Daedala (**Die**-da-la) 36

Dağbelen (**Daah**-bel-len) 11, 18, *59*, 64, 69-70, 73, *74*, 75

Dalaman (**Dal**-la-man) 36

Dalyan (**Dal**-yan) **17**, 34-5

Dandalaz (**Dan**-dal-laz) 28, 30

Datça (**Dat**-cha) 12, 32-3, *115*, **116**, *134*

Değirmenyanı (**Daay**-eer-men-yanuh) 32

Denizli (**Den**-eez-lee) 28-9, 39, 134

Dereköy (**Der**-reh-keuy) **17**, *58*, 76, 78-9

Dereözü (**De**-reh-euw-zeuw) *92*, 95, 98-9

Didim (**Dee**-deem) 22-3

Dörttepe (**Deuwrt**-tep-peh) 19

Ekindere (**Ek**-een-deh-reh) 21

Ephesus (**Ef**-fes-uhs) 15, 27, 38, 134

Eren Dağ (mountain) (**Ehr**-rehn **Daah**) 112, 114

Erine (**Ehr**-reen-eh) 12, *113*
Euromos (**Yew**-rom-moss) 20-1,
    23, 38-9

Fethiye (**Fet**-hee-yeh) 36-7, 134

Geriş (**Geh**-reesh) 57, *58*, 61,
    66-8
Gökçe (**Geuwk**-cheh) 34, 127,
    128, 129
Gökceler (**Geuwk**-jel-ler) 83, *85*
Gökova, Gulf of **18**, 35, 38, 98,
    118, *120*, 121, 123,
    125-27, 129
Gümbet (**Geuwm**-beht) 82, *85*
Gümüşlük (**Geuwm**-meuwsh-
    leuwk) 10, 16-17, 40,
    43, 53, *54*, 56, **cover**
Gündoğan (**Geuwn**-dooh-an) 11,
    16, 18, 73, *74*, 75
Güvercinlik (**Geuw**-ver-jeen-leek)
    16, 19, 20

Halicarnassus (**Ha**-li-carn-assus)
    83
Heraklia (**Her**-rak-leea) 20-2,
    25, 38-9
Hierapolis (**High**-ehr-apoliss) 28
Hisarönü (**Hee**-sahr-euwn-neuw)
    32, 112, *113*

Iassos (**I**-yass-oss) 21
İçmeler (**Eech**-mehl-lehr) 44,
    105-7, *110*, 133

Karabağ (**Ka**-ra-baah) 10, 16,
    49-50, *51*
Karakaya (**Ka**-ra-kie-ya) 10, 11,
    53, *54*, 55
Kargı (**Kahr**-guh) 12, *115*, 117
Kargıcak (**Kahr**-guh-jak) 86,
    87-8, *89*
Keçibükü (**Keht**-chee-beu-keu)
    111, *113*
Kibrel (**Kee**-brel) 69, **70**, 72, *74*
Knidos (**Knee**-doss) **32**, 33
Konacık (**Kon**-na-juhk) 11, 16,
    80, 81-3, *85*
Kuşadası (**Koosh**-ad-da-suh) 27

Labranda (**Lab**-ran-da) 20, 87-8,
    89, 90
Lagina (Temple of) (**La**-geen-ah)
    24-5

Marmaris (**Mar**-mar-rees) 7-9,
    11-12, 15, 32, 34-41,
    43, **90**, 91, *93*, 94, 97,
    99-104, **108**, 109, 112,
    118, 122, 126, 130-31,
    133, 134
    town plan *see touring map*
Milas (**Meel**-lass) 20, 31, 38-9,
    40, 86-8, *89*
Miletus (Milet) (**Meel**-let-tuhs)
    20, 22-3, 38-9
Muğla (**Moo**-la) 24, 28, 38-40,
    133
Mumcular (**Moom**-jool-ahr) 16,
    19

Ölü Deniz (**Oeul**-leu Den-neez)
    36
Orhaniye (**Or**-han-nee-yeh) 32,
    44, 111-12, *113*
Ortakent (**Or**-ta-kent) 16, 18,
    49, *59*, 62, **63**, 65-6, 68,
    76-7

Pamukkale (**Pam**-muh-kah-leh)
    15, 28-9, **30**, 39
Pedesa (**Ped**-ess-sa) 83-4, *85*, 86
Physcus (**Fiss**-coos) 11, 91, *93*
Priene (**Pree**-ehn-neh) 20, 23,
    38-9

Sandıma (**San**-duh-ma) 11, 18,
    57-8, *59*, 60, **61**, 62-3,
    64, 66, **67**
Sedir Adası (**Sed**-deer Ad-da-suh)
    18, 34-5, 121
Selçuk (**Sel**-chuhk) 27, 38-9
Side (**See**-deh) 69
Söke (**Seuw**-keh) 23, 27, 39

Tavas (**Ta**-vass) 29, 30
Telmessus (**Tel**-mess-soos) 36
Turgutreis (**Tuhr**-gut-re-ees) 10,
    16, 43, *51*
Turunç (**Tuhr**-ruhnch) 12, 44,
    104-5, 107-9, *110*

Yaka (**Ya**-ka) 18, 33, *59*, 62, 64,
    66, 68, 76-8
Yalıkavak (**Ya**-luh-ka-vak) 11,
    16, 18, 43, 57, *59*, 61,
    62, 63-4, 66-9, **67**
Yatağan (**Ya**-tah-ah-ahn) 24,
    28, 31, 38-40